עין לציון
Ayin L'Tziyon:
Looking Towards Zion

Edited by Karen L. Stein

Eitan Gutin, Contributing Author
Amy Greenfeld, Contributing Editor

United Synagogue of Conservative Judaism | Department of Youth Activities

UNITED SYNAGOGUE OF CONSERVATIVE JUDAISM

DEPARTMENT OF YOUTH ACTIVITIES

Jules A. Gutin	DIRECTOR
Karen L. Stein	ASSISTANT DIRECTOR
Aviva Tilles	PROJECTS DIRECTOR
Ilan Schwartz	PROGRAM COORDINATOR
Adam Kofinas	MEETINGS MANAGER
Amy Greenfeld	EDUCATION COORDINATOR
Matthew Halpern	COMMUNICATIONS COORDINATOR
Nahum Binder	CENTRAL SHALIACH
David Keren	DIRECTOR, ISRAEL PROGRAMS
Yitzchak Jacobsen	DIRECTOR, ISRAEL OFFICE
Yossi Garr	DIRECTOR, NATIV

INTERNATIONAL YOUTH COMMISSION
Paul Kochberg, CHAIRPERSON

UNITED SYNAGOGUE OF CONSERVATIVE JUDAISM
Dr. Ray Goldstein, INTERNATIONAL PRESIDENT
Rabbi Jerome M. Epstein, EXECUTIVE VICE-PRESIDENT
Dr. Marilyn Lishnoff Wind, VICE PRESIDENT FOR YOUTH SERVICES AND EDUCATION

A publication of the International Youth Commission
United Synagogue of Conservative Judaism
820 Second Avenue, New York, NY 10017
http://www.uscj.org/usy

First Edition, 2008

Printed and bound in the United States of America by Howard Press
Cover design by Matthew Halpern
Production, layout and design by Karen L. Stein, Project Editor

Table of Contents

Editor's Preface	4
Introduction	5
Prologue: My National Tefillah	7
PART ONE: BEING A ZIONIST	8
Defining Terms	9
Getting From Here to There	12
A Brit For Today	25
Because of our Sins	26
The Land that was Lost	31
Loss of Jerusalem = Exile	36
Living In The West	37
Hopes and Prayers	41
If He Tarries, I will wait	44
PART TWO: MODERN ZIONISM	50
God Helps Those	50
Zionism Reaches North America	56
Zionism and the Conservative Movement	57
The Jerusalem Program	63
Is Zionism Racism—Looking at the UN Resolution	66
Israel: A Look from the Diaspora	75
Is It A Mitzvah To Make Aliyah?	76
Does Israel Need Us?	83
What is the Place of Israel for North American Jews?	89
Tefillah L'shlom Hamedinah	92
Tikvateinu—Our Hope	95

Editor's Preface

לְמַעַן צִיּוֹן לֹא אֶחֱשֶׁה,
וּלְמַעַן יְרוּשָׁלַיִם לֹא אֶשְׁקוֹט,
עַד-יֵצֵא כַנֹּגַהּ צִדְקָהּ,
וִישׁוּעָתָהּ כְּלַפִּיד יִבְעָר.

For Zion's sake will I not hold remain silent,
and for Jerusalem's sake I will not be quiet,
until her triumph goes forth as brightness,
and her victory like a burning torch.
Isaiah 62:1

In May 2008, Israel celebrated its 60th birthday, a significant milestone that deserves special recognition and provides a great opportunity to celebrate its achievements and history.

This sourcebook focuses its attention on Jews in the Diaspora and our relationship with Israel. How can we strengthen our ties to Israel, while remaining connected to North America? Can we be true Zionists and not live in Israel?

This volume has benefited from the combined wisdom and experience of the talented individuals who contributed to this book. Eitan Gutin did a wonderful job bringing the texts from Tanakh to life—starting with the earliest connections to Eretz Yisrael through the more complicated relationships of exile and Galut. By presenting the background of Zionism and its founding fathers, Eitan allows us as readers to explore our own identity and create our own definitions of Zionism. Amy Greenfeld brought to the table modern texts and discussions on the questions of Diaspora Jewry and what our relationship to Israel needs to and should be. The combination of ancient and modernity illuminates the discussion, provokes thought and allows us, most importantly, to ask questions.

I am additionally grateful to Jules Gutin for the many important contributions to the questions and exercises in the book as well as Jonathan Greenberg's constructive comments and suggestions. Additionally, thank you to Nahum Binder for the attention to the Hebrew texts.

As we note in the second half of this book, the Conservative movement holds Zionism as one of its core principles since the movement was founded. We are grateful to Rabbi Jerome M. Epstein, Executive Vice President and Chief Executive Officer of the United Synagogue of Conservative Judaism for the introduction to this sourcebook. Rabbi Epstein has been the CEO of the USCJ since 1986 and Executive Vice President since 1989. As Rabbi Epstein concludes his term of service to the USCJ as Executive Vice President and CEO, we wish him mazal tov and best wishes—may he go from strength to strength.

Finally, I am grateful to my wonderful husband Adam for the best gift I have ever received and dedicate this book to our new son, Avi Benjamin Monaco who arrived on Shabbat, March 1, 2008.

Karen L. Stein, November, 2008

Introduction

Why We Care About Israel

by Rabbi Jerome M. Epstein

Israel is commemorating its 60th birthday, and Jews all over the world are celebrating. Most of us feel a sense of pride and joy over Israel's existence and its significant accomplishments during these past six decades.

Since its inception, the Conservative movement has been clear about the primacy of Israel. Israel is reflected in our hopes and in our prayers. We say "am Yisrael chai" (The nation of Israel will live) and "Israel is our homeland." Are these merely platitudes? What does it mean that Israel is important to us, if Israel's existence doesn't affect our life's choices? What is the importance of Israel to us if it doesn't influence our priorities? Indeed, if Israel doesn't shape the way we live it has minimal practical significance.

If Israel is important, it is important for us as a Conservative Jewish community to take a number of steps:

We must take advantage of the spiritual nourishment that only Israel can provide. Many Conservative Jews have spent time in Israel, but we as a movement must work actively to increase that number. A visit to Israel can nurture us. Taking advantage of Israel's educational and spiritual opportunities can nourish our souls. Walking in the land of our ancestors can touch us in a way that reading about those sites never will.

It is important for us to be consciously pro- Israel. That does not necessarily imply that we must refrain from challenging Israel to be better or to do things differently. Those who criticize or challenge are often attacked as being anti-Israel. Being pro-Israel means being engaged with Israel and wanting the best for it. At times, being pro-Israel may mean challenging particular actions or ideas, just as some one who is pro-Canada or pro-United States may challenge his or her country. As Jews we must engage with Israel, lovingly and sensitively, even if that occasionally pushes us to support it by challenging it.

We must be concerned about Israel's security, but we must be equally concerned about Israel's social fabric. The fact that so many Jews immigrate to Israel from distressed conditions puts extraordinary pressures on Israeli society. Successfully absorbing hundreds of thousands of Jews from the former Soviet Union and Ethiopia as well other disparate communities taxes Israel's resources. Because Israel is our homeland, we have a responsibility to help these new Israeli citizens reach their educational potential and develop their innate ability to contribute as full members of Israel's society. Coming from lands in which they may not have been given the tools to learn or may not have had the resources to sustain themselves challenges us to participate as Israel's partners in our investment in their future. They need special assistance and Israel needs our help to help them reach their potential. What a shame it would be to encourage them to find refuge in Israel's homeland and find that inadvertently a permanent underclass in Israel is created! We can make a difference!

We must be concerned about religious freedom in Israel just as we are throughout the world. The problem is more poignant in Israel because in Israel authentic Jews should be permitted to live authentic Judaism without state interference. Israel's chief rabbinate continues to harm those Jews who do not accept its authority. Jews who are not Orthodox often are denied their religious rights. Hundreds of thousands of people who wish to become Jews are denied the opportunity simply because they refuse to live the Orthodox life demanded by the chief rabbinate. We can make a difference if we will lift our voices to say that we recognize Israel as our homeland and we want rights for Conservative Jews as well as for Orthodox Jews. We must not be silent!

Although most Conservative Jews will live their lives in North America, as Israel celebrates its 60th year we must recognize that Israel was created to be a homeland for all Jews. As a movement we should encourage Conservative Jews to actively consider what aliyah would mean in their lives. With stimulation, there are those who will think deeply about the potential. In my mind, the challenge is not to pressure people to make aliyah but instead to encourage them to consider it as an opportunity or an alternative, either on a full time or a part time basis.

This USY sourcebook is designed to enable you to explore Israel's meaning in your life. Reading it is only the first step! Then we must let the ideas and sources we encounter shape our daily behavior and choices.

Israel's celebration is our celebration. May that celebration influence our lives.

Rabbi Jerome M. Epstein
Summer 2008

This article originally appeared in *CJ: Voices of Conservative/ Masorti Judaism*, Summer 2008.

Prologue - My National Tefillah - תְּפִלָּה

Each of us has a special, personal way to express our individual hopes, dreams, and needs. Sometimes we choose an art, such as music or painting. Many of us write, whether in something private like a journal or public like a blog. Some of us never have any sort of permanent, personal record of our wishes - instead, we express them in conversations with friends and family, or just think about them as we lie in bed at night, ready to go to sleep.

Among the Jewish people, whenever there is a shared national wish or need, we express ourselves in the words of tefillah (Jewish prayer). To read any of the books that contain tefillah such as the Siddur or Haggadah, is to be exposed to a snapshot of the priorities of B'nei Yisrael at a given moment in time. Each generation for over 2000 years has added its stamp to the Siddur and other texts that contain tefillot.

Today, it is your turn. What do you think the Jewish people need right now? What should be our communal focus in the years to come?

Take a moment to think about your answers to the above questions, and then use the box below to write a tefillah for the needs of the Jewish people:

Part One- Being a Zionist

> **"ERETZ-ISRAEL** was the birthplace of the Jewish people.
> Here their spiritual, religious and political identity was shaped.
> Here they first attained to statehood, created cultural values of
> national and universal significance and gave to the world the
> eternal Book of Books.
>
> After being forcibly exiled from their land, the people kept faith
> with it throughout their scattering to different lands, and never
> ceased to pray and hope for their return to their land and re-
> establish their political freedom."

These words, read by David Ben-Gurion just after 4 PM, Erev Shabbat, the 14th of May 1948, ushered in a new era of Jewish history. The statements made in these first two paragraphs covered thousands of years of the Jewish experience, including the nearly 2000 years between the destruction of the second Temple in Jerusalem and the founding of the Jewish State.

There is no way to properly capture, or even begin to understand, 2000 years of struggle and hope. You could say, for example, that when the United States declared independence in 1776, our ancestors had been already been spread throughout the world for 1700 years; or when Gutenberg invented the first printing press in 1439, the basic form and text of the Siddur (which was a substitute for Temple ritual) had already been around for at least 600 years; Even England, one of the oldest countries in the world, has only been around for half of the time that we were in Exile.

When countries and nations were rising and falling around us, and when we as a people went through constant cycles of acceptance and rejection by those nations, there was one idea, and one idea only, that kept us going - that we, the Jewish people, had a special promise from *Adonai* that there was a home for us in the world and that one day we would return. Our hope sustained us, and, on that Erev Shabbat in May of 1948, gave birth to the modern State of Israel.

Defining Terms:

There are a number of Hebrew terms and phrases used throughout this sourcebook.

When speaking and learning about Israel, understanding the difference between one label or another can be very important. What follows are a few of the more important phrases and concepts that you will be exposed to while you learn about our homeland:

Israel— Yisrael

The name given to *Ya'akov* (Jacob) after he wrestles with a "Man of God" all night. The name is part of a blessing *that Ya'akov* demands from the man in order to release him. Sort of an ancient form of demanding that he "cry uncle." The names *Yisrael* and *Ya'akov* are used interchangeably throughout the rest of the Torah. It can also be used as a short way of referring to the entire Jewish people.
For example - "All of Israel is responsible for one another." (Talmud Shavuot 39a)

Children of Israel *B'nei Yisrael*

Initially refers to the immediate offspring of *Ya'akov* – his 12 sons, daughters, and their children as well. The first time the phrase is used to refer to the Jewish nation, it is written as "The nation of the children of *Yisrael*," as if to make a distinction between the immediate sons of *Ya'akov* and the nation that they become over multiple generations (*Shmot*, chapter 1, verse 9) From that point on, the Jewish nation is known as B'nei Yisrael. This still holds true today when we speak about ourselves as a nation. This term can also be Am Yisrael which literally means the "Nation of Israel." This sourcebook will generally use B'nei Yisrael unless quoting directly from a text that uses another title.

The Land of Israel *Eretz Yisrael*

The land promised by God in the Torah to *Avraham, Yitzhak, Ya'akov*, and eventually all of B'nei Yisrael. As you will see later in this book, there is some debate as to actually how much territory can be referred to as Eretz Yisrael.

The State of Israel *Medinat Yirael*

The modern Jewish state that exists on a large chunk (but not all of) Eretz Yisrael.
You do not need to be a member of B'nei Yisrael to be considered a citizen of Eretz Yisrael.

Activity: Israel and Me

For each of the following statements, circle the number that most reflects your opinion. On the line below each statement, take a moment to write any examples you think of based on the statement:

	Strongly Agree	Agree	Not Sure/ Neutral	Dis-agree	Strongly Disagree
1) I am a Zionist.	1	2	3	4	5
Examples:					
2) As a Jew, I should support the decisions of the Israeli government.	1	2	3	4	5
Examples:					
3) Israeli music is automatically Jewish music.	1	2	3	4	5
Examples:					
4) By living in North America, I am living in the *Galut,* exile from the Jewish homeland of Israel.	1	2	3	4	5
Examples:					
5) There is no conflict between being a patriotic American/ Canadian, and supporting *Medinat Yisrael,* the State of Israel, even when the governments might disagree.	1	2	3	4	5
Examples:					
6) Israel is inspirational.	1	2	3	4	5
Examples:					
7) There is a Jewish right to *Eretz Yisrael,* the Land of Israel, because of promises God made to our ancestors.	1	2	3	4	5
Examples:					
8) Since it is the Jewish State, it makes sense for Israeli law to be influenced by Jewish law.	1	2	3	4	5
Examples:					

	Strongly Agree	Agree	Not Sure/ Neutral	Dis-agree	Strongly Disagree
9) It is important to follow Israeli news on a regular basis.	1	2	3	4	5
Examples:					
10) With safe places to live such as the US, Canada, and Great Britain, Medinat Yisrael is no longer necessary for the safety of the Jewish people.	1	2	3	4	5
Examples:					
11) It is impossible to understand Medinat Yisrael without having contact with Israeli Jews.	1	2	3	4	5
Examples:					
12) I should speak out when I disagree with the decisions of the Israeli government.	1	2	3	4	5
Examples:					
13) God takes a direct interest, and exerts influence, on the modern State of Israel.	1	2	3	4	5
Examples:					
14) *Tzahal*– The Israeli Defense Forces or IDF, is the Jewish people's army.	1	2	3	4	5
Examples:					
15) It is important to travel to Eretz Yisrael.	1	2	3	4	5
Examples:					
16) "Anti-Israel" is the same thing as "anti-Jewish"	1	2	3	4	5
Examples:					
17) Zionism was important once, but does not really matter anymore.	1	2	3	4	5
Examples:					
18) Every Jew in the world should make *Aliyah*, "going up", moving to Israel	1	2	3	4	5
Examples:					

Getting from there to here

In North America there is often talk of "patriotism," especially during big election years. A patriot is someone who loves his country, and will defend it fiercely when challenged. While patriotism is about internalized ideas and beliefs, it also often involves specific actions - from tangible ones such as voting to more ritualistic ones like singing the National Anthem.

What if you are part of a people with a long history and tradition, but without a home, wandering around the world for 2000 years? Can one be patriotic in the absence of a country to be patriotic about?

After centuries of hoping and praying for a return to Eretz Yisrael, many Jews in 19th century Europe were ready for a change. They were tired of being a homeless nation within a nation.

Some decided it was time to abandon the idea of a Jewish homeland - France, England, Germany, or the United States would be the homeland of the Jews who lived there.

Others, however, took the opposite track, deciding that it was time to take the hopes and prayers of countless generations and turn them into action - it was time to go back and reclaim the land of our ancestors. **Zionism** was an ideology the likes of which the world had never experienced before in which a people with a common history, but spread to the four corners of the Earth, banded together and said with one clear voice: "it is time for us to go home."

In The Beginning...

In order to form an understanding of what Medinat Yisrael is all about, it is essential to look at the beliefs and history that took us from a single family of nomads 4000 years ago to the nation we have become today.

TEXT 1	
לִבִּי בְמִזְרָח וְאָנֹכִי בְּסוֹף מַעֲרָב	My heart is in the East and I am at the edge of the West
אֵיךְ אֶטְעֲמָה אֶת אֲשֶׁר אֹכַל וְאֵיךְ יֶעֱרָב	How can I savor my food? How can it be sweet to me?
אֵיכָה אֲשַׁלֵּם נְדָרַי וֶאֱסָרַי, בְּעוֹד	How can I deliver on my vows and promises, while
צִיּוֹן בְּחֶבֶל אֱדוֹם וַאֲנִי בְּכֶבֶל עֲרָב	Zion is bound by Edom (Rome), and I in Arab chains?
יֵקַל בְּעֵינַי עֲזֹב כָּל טוֹב סְפָרַד, כְּמוֹ	In my eyes, it would be easy to leave all the good things in Spain --
יֵקַר בְּעֵינַי רְאוֹת עַפְרוֹת דְּבִיר נֶחֱרָב.	Seeing how precious it would be in my eyes to behold the dust of the desolate sanctuary.

by Yehuda HaLevi (c. 1080-1142). Translation adapted from http://www.angelfire.com/ct/halevi

When have you wanted something so much that it kept you from noticing what you were eating, what someone was saying to you, or what you were watching on TV? Why did it distract you so much?

In his time, HaLevi's home of Spain was a place in which Jews were a regular part of everyday society. The Jewish community was just about as free then, nearly 1000 years ago, as we are today in North America. Why, then, do you think HaLevi referred to his being in "Arab chains?"

What "vows and promises" do you think HaLevi is talking about? What sort of promises can only be fulfilled in Eretz Yisrael?

Those of us who live in North America are citizens of countries in which we are free, and our rights are protected by the government. Is it appropriate to constantly talk about, study, discuss, and even hope to move to Israel given how well we as Jews have been treated by the US and Canada?

For generations before and after Yehuda HaLevi lived, there was one dream of the Jewish people – to return to our homeland, Eretz Yisrael. The idea of Eretz Yisrael as the homeland of B'nei Yisrael can be traced all the way back to the Torah in which special promises about this piece of land were made to Abraham, Isaac, Jacob, and eventually everyone in Am Yisrael.

Avraham

Without Avraham and his willingness to follow wherever God led him, no matter what, there might not be a story that includes the Jewish people. From the very first encounter we have with his story, when God says go, Avraham goes.

From the moment God says to go, however, there are promises. For example, right after the famous moment when God says "Lech Lecha" (go), God makes some guarantees:

TEXT 2

ב - וְאֶעֶשְׂךָ, לְגוֹי גָּדוֹל וַאֲבָרֶכְךָ וַאֲגַדְּלָה שְׁמֶךָ וֶהְיֵה, בְּרָכָה

2 - I will make of you a great nation, And I will bless you; I will make your name great, And you shall be a blessing.

ג - וַאֲבָרְכָה, מְבָרְכֶיךָ וּמְקַלֶּלְךָ, אָאֹר וְנִבְרְכוּ בְךָ, כֹּל מִשְׁפְּחֹת הָאֲדָמָה

3 – I will bless those who bless you And curse anyone that curses you And all the families of the earth shall bless themselves by you...

בראשית י"ב:ב-ג   *Bereishit Chapter 12, verses 2-3*

How important is the Torah to our understanding of just what Eretz Yisrael means? Let's take a look at the promises God made to our ancestors, and piece together from the Torah the special place Eretz Yisrael holds in the collective hearts of B'nei Yisrael.

Why do you think God makes these guarantees to Avraham as part of the request, or command, to "go"? Shouldn't the word of God be enough?

Once promises are being made, shouldn't it be sufficient to be a "great nation"? Why do you think God adds the promises in Verse 3 about blessings and curses?

While there are a number of key moments when God makes promises to our ancestors, this is the original. Why do you think God offers these promises first?

In the situation on the previous page, there is already a give and take between God and Avraham. Yes, God is guaranteeing future results for Avraham, but (at least at this moment) on one condition – that Avraham go where God tells him to.

Of course, we know the story form this point. Avraham follows God's instructions, and ends up settling his family in the future Eretz Yisrael (which for most of the Torah is known as Canaan). Here we have the first mention in our text of the "Promised Land," a special place on Earth set aside by God for the use of all the generations Avraham will eventually produce:

TEXT 3

ז - וַיֵּרָא יְהוָה, אֶל-אַבְרָם, וַיֹּאמֶר לְזַרְעֲךָ אֶתֵּן אֶת-הָאָרֶץ הַזֹּאת

Adonai appeared to Abram and said, "I will give this land to your descendants."

בראשית י"ב:ז   Bereishit Chapter 12, Verse 7

God has already promised Avraham all sorts of things. Why add land into the mix? Especially a land that will have to be fought for, multiple times, in future generations?

What do you think the promises made by God in Texts 2 and 3 tell us about what Avraham thought was valuable? If God were making promises to someone today, do you think they would be similar to Avraham's or something noticeably different?

What other questions do you have that might help you to understand this text?

Once he is settled, and has worked things out with his nephew, Lot, Avraham gets involved in a war – it is Avraham against five kings, and he eventually emerges victorious. After this life or death experience, he starts to question just what will happen to his wealth and success when he dies. Keep in mind that, in ancient times the definition of success for an individual, particularly a male head-of-household, was property. Anything you had worked for and accumulated while alive was to be passed on to your male child or children - which Avraham had yet to produce!

There is an exchange between God and Avraham about his worries in chapter 15 of *Bereishit:*

TEXT 4

א - אַחַר הַדְּבָרִים הָאֵלֶּה, הָיָה דְבַר-יְהֹוָה אֶל-אַבְרָם, בַּמַּחֲזֶה, לֵאמֹר אַל-תִּירָא אַבְרָם, אָנֹכִי מָגֵן לָךְ--שְׂכָרְךָ, הַרְבֵּה מְאֹד

1 Some time later, the word of *Adonai* came to Abram in a vision. God said, "Fear not, Abram, I am a shield to you; Your reward shall be very great."

ב - וַיֹּאמֶר אַבְרָם, אֲדֹנָי יְהוִה מַה-תִּתֶּן-לִי, וְאָנֹכִי, הוֹלֵךְ עֲרִירִי; וּבֶן-מֶשֶׁק בֵּיתִי, הוּא דַּמֶּשֶׂק אֱלִיעֶזֶר

2 But Abram replied, "*Adonai,* God, what can You give me, seeing that I shall die childless, and the one in charge of my household is d*ammesek** Eliezer!"

ג - וַיֹּאמֶר אַבְרָם--הֵן לִי, לֹא נָתַתָּה זָרַע; וְהִנֵּה בֶן-בֵּיתִי, יוֹרֵשׁ אֹתִי.

3 Abram said further, "Since You have granted me no offspring, my servant will be my heir."

ד - וְהִנֵּה דְבַר-יְהֹוָה אֵלָיו לֵאמֹר, לֹא יִירָשְׁךָ זֶה כִּי-אִם אֲשֶׁר יֵצֵא מִמֵּעֶיךָ, הוּא יִירָשֶׁךָ

4 The word of *Adonai* came to him in reply, "That one shall not be your heir; none but your very own issue shall be your heir."

ה - וַיּוֹצֵא אֹתוֹ הַחוּצָה, וַיֹּאמֶר הַבֶּט-נָא הַשָּׁמַיְמָה וּסְפֹר הַכּוֹכָבִים אִם-תּוּכַל לִסְפֹּר אֹתָם ; וַיֹּאמֶר לוֹ, כֹּה יִהְיֶה זַרְעֶךָ

5 God took him outside and said, "Look toward heaven and count the stars, see if you are able to count them." And God added, "So shall your offspring be."

ו - וְהֶאֱמִן, בַּיהֹוָה; וַיַּחְשְׁבֶהָ לּוֹ, צְדָקָה

6 Because he put his trust in *Adonai,* God reckoned it to his merit.

ז - וַיֹּאמֶר, אֵלָיו: אֲנִי יְהֹוָה, אֲשֶׁר הוֹצֵאתִיךָ מֵאוּר כַּשְׂדִּים לָתֶת לְךָ אֶת-הָאָרֶץ הַזֹּאת, לְרִשְׁתָּהּ

7 Then God said to him, "I am *Adonai* who brought you out from Ur of the Chaldeans to give this land to you to posses."

At this point the text continues, with a complex set of offerings Avram has to perform.

God then tells Avram that, in the future, his descendants will be "strangers in a land that is not theirs," and eventually end up as slaves.

After describing 400 years of slavery, and the eventual escape, the text continues:

י"ח - בַּיּוֹם הַהוּא, כָּרַת יְהֹוָה אֶת-אַבְרָם—בְּרִית לֵאמֹר לְזַרְעֲךָ, נָתַתִּי אֶת-הָאָרֶץ הַזֹּאת, מִנְּהַר מִצְרַיִם, עַד-הַנָּהָר הַגָּדֹל נְהַר-פְּרָת

18 On that day *Adonai* made a **covenant** with Abram, saying, "To your offspring I assign this land, from the river of Egypt to the great river, the river Euphrates..."

בראשית ט"ו:א-ז, י"ח   *Bereishit, chapter 15, verses 1-7, and 18*

*it is unclear what this word means here. It used to be translated as "Eliezer from Damascus," but the grammar does not support that translation. Others think this is one example of the biblical version of a typo. Modern translations just write in the Hebrew word.

Why do you think Avraham has become so nervous? Why might he be having trouble trusting that God's previous promise, that he will produce a great nation?

Remember that God made the promise earlier that Avraham would be a "great nation." What do you think the meaning is behind God's use of visuals – the stars in the night sky – to reassert this point?

What do you think God expects out of Avraham, in exchange for all these promises?

What other questions do you have that might help you to understand this text?

Chapter 15 of *Bereishit* introduces us to a concept that has remained vital to Jewish belief from Biblical times until today – the idea that there is a **Brit** a special "covenant" between God and the Jewish people, that is somehow centered on Eretz Yisrael.

Just what is a **covenant**? Sometimes, it is helpful to think of it as a special type of **contract** between us, the Jewish people, and God. Lawyers use the word in just this way – a covenant is a contract that deals with land ownership or rights – which is basically what the Brit between us and God is all about.

There are all sorts of situations you will encounter in life that require a contract. While we all usually think of contracts as being legal documents, a contract is any two-way agreement between two or more people. For examples, if your parents promise to get you a new iPod if you have an A average at the end of the school year, and you agree, that is a basic contract.

Activity: Creating Covenants

What sort of "covenants" are you a part of...

Between you and your parents

Between you and your school

Between you and your community

Between you and your country

Between you and God

List below some personal examples of those covenants:

Activity: Comparing Covenants I

Based on what you already know about the Brit, fill in God and Avraham's respective obligations below:

GOD	AVRAHAM

From the very beginning Avraham's relationship with God is a two-way street. It is clear that God expects Avraham to follow God's instructions. However, on multiple occasions God makes it clear that there is a reward for Avraham's choice to follow – a promised reward of a great nation, and a land for the Jewish people to call their own.

At key moments in the development of our people's story, God restates or re-establishes the Brit for a new generation. Over time, the Brit changes, incorporating new details and new situations. At the same time, the relationship between God and B'nei Yisrael gets increasingly complex. What follows are two important developments in the Brit ,one from Avraham's grandson, Ya'akov, the other from the time B'nei Yisrael spends in the desert on the way to Eretz Yisrael from Egypt.

After each set of texts, you will once again be asked to fill in the terms of the Brit:

Ya'acov

This takes place while Ya'akov is on the run after getting the blessing meant for his brother, Esav. He finds a place to sleep for the night, and has a dream in which Mal'akhim (angels) were going up and down ladders. It is during the dream that God speaks:

TEXT 5

י"ג - וַיֹּאמַר, אֲנִי יְהוָה אֱלֹהֵי אַבְרָהָם אָבִיךָ, וֵאלֹהֵי יִצְחָק. הָאָרֶץ, אֲשֶׁר אַתָּה שֹׁכֵב עָלֶיהָ--לְךָ אֶתְּנֶנָּה, וּלְזַרְעֶךָ.

13 God said, "I am Adonai, the God of your father Abraham and the God of Isaac: the ground on which you are lying I will assign to you and to your offspring.

י"ד - וְהָיָה זַרְעֲךָ כַּעֲפַר הָאָרֶץ, וּפָרַצְתָּ יָמָּה וָקֵדְמָה וְצָפֹנָה וָנֶגְבָּה וְנִבְרְכוּ בְךָ כָּל-מִשְׁפְּחֹת הָאֲדָמָה, וּבְזַרְעֶךָ.

14 Your descendants shall be as the dust of the earth; you shall spread out to the west and to the east, to the north and to the south. All the families of the earth shall bless themselves by you and your descendants.

ט"ו - וְהִנֵּה אָנֹכִי עִמָּךְ, וּשְׁמַרְתִּיךָ בְּכֹל אֲשֶׁר-תֵּלֵךְ, וַהֲשִׁבֹתִיךָ, אֶל-הָאֲדָמָה הַזֹּאת כִּי, לֹא אֶעֱזָבְךָ, עַד אֲשֶׁר אִם-עָשִׂיתִי, אֵת אֲשֶׁר-דִּבַּרְתִּי לָךְ.

15 Remember, I am with you: I will protect you wherever you go and will bring you back to this land. I will not leave you until I have done what I have promised you."

At this point, deciding he is in a special, holy place, Ya'akov sets up a monument establishing this location as Beit El, the "House of God." He then goes on to make the following promise:

כ - אִם-יִהְיֶה אֱלֹהִים עִמָּדִי, וּשְׁמָרַנִי בַּדֶּרֶךְ הַזֶּה אֲשֶׁר אָנֹכִי הוֹלֵךְ וְנָתַן-לִי לֶחֶם לֶאֱכֹל, וּבֶגֶד לִלְבֹּשׁ.

20 If God remains with me, if He protects me on this journey that I am making, and gives me bread to eat and clothing to wear,

כ"א - וְשַׁבְתִּי בְשָׁלוֹם, אֶל-בֵּית אָבִי; וְהָיָה יְהוָה לִי, לֵאלֹהִים.

21 and if I return safe to my father's house – *Adonai* shall be my God.

בראשית כ"ח:י"ג-י"ד, כ-כ"א | *Bereishit, chapter 28, verses 13-15, 20, 21*

What similarities do you see between the Brit as God presents it to Ya'akov, and the Brit made with Avraham? What is new, or different? Why do you think Ya'akov and Avraham hear different versions of what seems to be the same thing?

What do you think God means when God says "I will not leave you?" Does the Brit have a time limit?

How is the way Ya'akov deals with God different from the example set by Avraham? What does he add to the Brit that was missing previously?

Activity: Comparing Covenants II

Before continuing, and based on what you know about the Brit, fill in God and Ya'akov's obligations below:

GOD	Ya'akov

By declaring, in verse 21, that "*Adonai* **shall be**" his God, Ya'akov establishes a new phase in the relationship between God and the Jewish people. Up until Ya'akov, those in the Torah who interacted with God did whatever they were told without conditions. Yes, promises were made, but the exchanges between God and Avraham, for example, were basically one-sided. Even when Avraham does get involved in the conversation about his future, he does so without making a direct request to God. Instead, as we read in chapter 15 of *Bereishit* (Text 4) Avraham shares his worries and fears with God. Compare this to Ya'akov, who lays out conditions for his following God, and making *Adonai* his personal deity. As you will see, it is this conditional relationship that becomes the model for the Jewish people's Brit in the future.

B'nei Yisrael

When *Yosef* brings his father Ya'akov and brothers with him to live in Egypt, it begins a new chapter in the history of our people. We grow beyond the confines of being a single family, and for the first time establish our identity as a nation. Soon after achieving this growth, we are bound up as slaves and, for hundreds of years, know nothing but pain and suffering. If not for God's presence, and *Adonai*'s listening to our cries our history would have ended on the banks of the Nile; instead, *Adonai* fulfilled the Brit with *Avraham, Yitzhak* and *Ya'akov,* breaking our chains, eventually

TEXT 6

ב וַיְדַבֵּר אֱלֹהִים, אֶל-מֹשֶׁה; וַיֹּאמֶר אֵלָיו, אֲנִי יְהוָה	2 God spoke to Moses and said to him, "I am *Adonai*.
ג וָאֵרָא, אֶל-אַבְרָהָם אֶל-יִצְחָק וְאֶל-יַעֲקֹב-בְּאֵל שַׁדָּי; וּשְׁמִי יְהוָה, לֹא נוֹדַעְתִּי לָהֶם	3 I appeared to Abraham, Isaac, and Jacob as *El Shaddai*, but I did not make Myself known to them by My name YHWH*
ד וְגַם הֲקִמֹתִי אֶת-בְּרִיתִי אִתָּם, לָתֵת לָהֶם אֶת-אֶרֶץ כְּנָעַן--אֵת אֶרֶץ מְגֻרֵיהֶם, אֲשֶׁר-גָּרוּ בָהּ	4 I also established My covenant with them, to give them the land of Canaan, the land in which they lived as sojourners.
ה וְגַם אֲנִי שָׁמַעְתִּי, אֶת-נַאֲקַת בְּנֵי יִשְׂרָאֵל, אֲשֶׁר מִצְרַיִם, מַעֲבִדִים אֹתָם; וָאֶזְכֹּר, אֶת-בְּרִיתִי	5 I have now heard the moaning of the Israelites because the Egyptians are holding them in bondage, and I have remembered My covenant.
ו לָכֵן אֱמֹר לִבְנֵי-יִשְׂרָאֵל, אֲנִי יְהוָה, וְהוֹצֵאתִי אֶתְכֶם מִתַּחַת סִבְלֹת מִצְרַיִם, וְהִצַּלְתִּי אֶתְכֶם מֵעֲבֹדָתָם; וְגָאַלְתִּי אֶתְכֶם בִּזְרוֹעַ נְטוּיָה, וּבִשְׁפָטִים גְּדֹלִים	6 Say, therefore, to the Israelite people: I am *Adonai*. I will free you from the labors of the Egyptians and deliver you from their bondage. I will redeem you with an outstretched arm and through extraordinary chastisements.
ז וְלָקַחְתִּי אֶתְכֶם לִי לְעָם, וְהָיִיתִי לָכֶם לֵאלֹהִים; וִידַעְתֶּם, כִּי אֲנִי יְהוָה אֱלֹהֵיכֶם, הַמּוֹצִיא אֶתְכֶם, מִתַּחַת סִבְלוֹת מִצְרָיִם	7 And I will take you to be My people, and I will be your God. And you shall know that I, *Adonai*, am your God who freed you from the labors of the Egyptians.

*While most of the time יהוה has been translated the way we pronounce it, as "Adonai," at this moment in the text God is making a point that יהוה is a special name. Therefore, the translation writes out the letters of the name in English, as YHWH.

ח וְהֵבֵאתִי אֶתְכֶם, אֶל-הָאָרֶץ, אֲשֶׁר נָשָׂאתִי אֶת-יָדִי, לָתֵת אֹתָהּ לְאַבְרָהָם לְיִצְחָק וּלְיַעֲקֹב; וְנָתַתִּי אֹתָהּ לָכֶם מוֹרָשָׁה, אֲנִי יְהֹוָה

8 I will bring you into the land which I swore to give to Abraham, Isaac, and Jacob, and I will give it to you for a possession, I *Adonai*."

ט וַיְדַבֵּר מֹשֶׁה כֵּן, אֶל-בְּנֵי יִשְׂרָאֵל; וְלֹא שָׁמְעוּ, אֶל-מֹשֶׁה, מִקֹּצֶר רוּחַ, וּמֵעֲבֹדָה קָשָׁה

9 But when Moses told this to the Israelites, they would not listen to Moses, their spirits crushed by cruel bondage.

שמות ו:ב-ט   *Shmot chapter 6, verses 2-9*

Take a look at verses 2 and 3 on the previous page - Why should it be important to Moshe and the rest of B'nei Yisrael that God uses a name here that was not "revealed" to their ancestors?

One of our concepts of God is that God is omniscient, which means all-knowing. Why would an omniscient God only notice the suffering of B'nei Yisrael when they "moan" (verse 5), and only then remember the Brit?

What might be a possible link between verse 7 and the conditions Ya'akov places on his relationship with God?

B'nei Yisrael were slaves for hundreds of years. Why does God wait so long to come through on the promises made to Avraham, Yitzhak, and Ya'akov?

What other questions might help you understand this text?

_____

_____

_____

_____

An important concept is first introduced to Jewish belief in verse 6 of the above text – the concept of *Ge'ulah*. The word translates as "redemption," and in Jewish belief refers to any time that B'nei Yisrael have been taken out of Eretz Yisrael and God brings us back. The belief in ge'ulah and how it works, plays a major role in Jewish beliefs and opinions about both Eretz Yisrael and Medinat Yisrael.

The Brit does not begin to go through any major transformations until B'nei Yisrael are traveling through the desert, on their way to the "promised land." On multiple occasions God outlines what is required in order to remain, undisturbed, in Eretz Yisrael ,or what behaviors will get B'nei Yisrael exiled from of the land for a period of time. Here are a few examples of how the Brit develops while B'nei Yisrael are wandering in the desert:

TEXT 7
B'nei Yisrael have just arrived at Mt. Sinai, and God begins to give instructions to Moshe:

ג - כֹּה תֹאמַר לְבֵית יַעֲקֹב, וְתַגֵּיד לִבְנֵי יִשְׂרָאֵל	3 "Thus shall you say to the house of Jacob and declare to the children of Israel:
ד - אַתֶּם רְאִיתֶם, אֲשֶׁר עָשִׂיתִי לְמִצְרָיִם; וָאֶשָּׂא אֶתְכֶם עַל-כַּנְפֵי נְשָׁרִים, וָאָבִא אֶתְכֶם אֵלָי	4 'You have seen what I did to the Egyptians, how I bore you on eagles' wings and brought you to Me.
ה - וְעַתָּה, אִם-שָׁמוֹעַ תִּשְׁמְעוּ בְּקֹלִי, וּשְׁמַרְתֶּם, אֶת-בְּרִיתִי וִהְיִיתֶם לִי סְגֻלָּה מִכָּל-הָעַמִּים, כִּי-לִי כָּל-הָאָרֶץ	5 Now then, if you will obey Me faithfully and keep My covenant, you shall be My treasured possession among all the peoples. Indeed, all the earth is Mine...

שמות י"ט:ג-ה   *Shmot chapter 19, verses 3-5*

TEXT 8
One of the most direct statements that can be considered part of the Brit is in the 10 "statements," the one about honoring parents:

י"א - כַּבֵּד אֶת-אָבִיךָ, וְאֶת-אִמֶּךָ לְמַעַן, יַאֲרִכוּן יָמֶיךָ, עַל הָאֲדָמָה, אֲשֶׁר-יְהֹוָה אֱלֹהֶיךָ נֹתֵן לָךְ	11 Honor your father and your mother, that your days will be long on **the land** that *Adonai* your God is giving to you.

שמות כ:י"א   *Shmot chapter 20, verse 11*

What changes about the Brit in Texts 7 and 8?

What is the result if B'nei Yisrael do not obey God that is implied by verse 5 in Text 7?

What do you think God means when God says the result of honoring your parents will be that "your days will be long on the land *Adonai* your God is giving to you"?

What other questions can you think of that might help you to understand these texts?

_____

_____

_____

It is in the book of *D'varim*, during Moshe's final speech to the people, that the Brit and the way it connects B'nei Yisrael to Eretz Yisrael is truly laid out in detail. While the language and details change from telling to telling, one message is clear – our success, as a people, in Eretz Yisrael is directly related to whether or not we are following God's will.

Even though it is read every day in *Shaharit* and *Ma'ariv*, we very rarely take a close look at this text from *D'varim*, chapter 11. It is one of the clearest presentations of the terms of the Brit that can be found in the Torah:

TEXT 9

יג וְהָיָה, אִם-שָׁמֹעַ תִּשְׁמְעוּ אֶל-מִצְוֹתַי, אֲשֶׁר אָנֹכִי מְצַוֶּה אֶתְכֶם, הַיּוֹם--לְאַהֲבָה אֶת-יְהוָה אֱלֹהֵיכֶם, וּלְעָבְדוֹ, בְּכָל-לְבַבְכֶם, וּבְכָל-נַפְשְׁכֶם

13 If, then, you obey the commandments that I enjoin upon you this day, loving *Adonai* your God and serving God with all your heart and soul,

יד וְנָתַתִּי מְטַר-אַרְצְכֶם בְּעִתּוֹ, יוֹרֶה וּמַלְקוֹשׁ; וְאָסַפְתָּ דְגָנֶךָ, וְתִירֹשְׁךָ וְיִצְהָרֶךָ

14 I will grant the rain for your land in season, the early rain and the late. You shall gather in your new grain and wine and oil --

טו וְנָתַתִּי עֵשֶׂב בְּשָׂדְךָ, לִבְהֶמְתֶּךָ; וְאָכַלְתָּ, וְשָׂבָעְתָּ

15 I will also provide grass in the fields for your cattle -- and thus you shall eat your fill.

טז הִשָּׁמְרוּ לָכֶם, פֶּן יִפְתֶּה לְבַבְכֶם; וְסַרְתֶּם, וַעֲבַדְתֶּם אֱלֹהִים אֲחֵרִים, וְהִשְׁתַּחֲוִיתֶם, לָהֶם

16 Take care not to be lured away to serve other gods and bow to them.

יז וְחָרָה אַף-יְהוָה בָּכֶם, וְעָצַר אֶת-הַשָּׁמַיִם וְלֹא-יִהְיֶה מָטָר, וְהָאֲדָמָה, לֹא תִתֵּן אֶת-יְבוּלָהּ; וַאֲבַדְתֶּם מְהֵרָה, מֵעַל הָאָרֶץ הַטֹּבָה, אֲשֶׁר יְהוָה, נֹתֵן לָכֶם

17 For *Adonai*'s anger will flare up against you, and God will shut up the skies so that there will be no rain and the ground will not yield its produce; and you will soon perish from the good land that Adonai is assigning to you

יח וְשַׂמְתֶּם אֶת-דְּבָרַי אֵלֶּה, עַל-לְבַבְכֶם וְעַל-נַפְשְׁכֶם; וּקְשַׁרְתֶּם אֹתָם לְאוֹת עַל-יֶדְכֶם, וְהָיוּ לְטוֹטָפֹת בֵּין עֵינֵיכֶם

18 Therefore impress these, My words, upon your very heart: bind them as a sign on your hand and let them serve as a symbol on your forehead,

יט וְלִמַּדְתֶּם אֹתָם אֶת-בְּנֵיכֶם, לְדַבֵּר בָּם, בְּשִׁבְתְּךָ בְּבֵיתֶךָ וּבְלֶכְתְּךָ בַדֶּרֶךְ, וּבְשָׁכְבְּךָ וּבְקוּמֶךָ

19 and teach them to your children -- reciting them when you stay at home and when you are away, when you lie down and when you get up;

כ וּכְתַבְתָּם עַל-מְזוּזוֹת בֵּיתֶךָ, וּבִשְׁעָרֶיךָ

20 and inscribe them on the doorposts of your house and on your gates --

כא לְמַעַן יִרְבּוּ יְמֵיכֶם, וִימֵי בְנֵיכֶם, עַל הָאֲדָמָה, אֲשֶׁר נִשְׁבַּע יְהוָה לַאֲבֹתֵיכֶם לָתֵת לָהֶם--כִּימֵי הַשָּׁמַיִם, עַל-הָאָרֶץ

21 to the end that you and your children may endure, in the land that *Adonai* swore to your fathers to give to them, as long as there is a heaven over the earth.

דברים י"א:י"ג-כ"א   *D'varim chapter 11, verses 13-21*

If it were up to you, which of the Mitzvot (commandments) would be the ones that are the most important for B'nei Yisrael to fulfill the terms of the Brit?

Why is the reward not only the land, but also rain at the right time and production of grain, wine, and oil? Since in the other texts we studied, God did not go much beyond promising the land, why does God go further here?

Is there a link between rain and being able to keep the land away from our enemies? Whether or not such a link existed in biblical times, might it exist today?

If we follow God's Mitzvot in general, we not only get the land but also rain. If we begin to worship other gods, which is a violation of one specific Mitzvah, that is when God will stop the rains. With all the laws to choose from, why do you think God specifically chose worshipping other gods as a trigger for punishing B'nei Yisrael?

According the verse 21, what is the reason given why B'nei Yisrael should follow God's laws?

Having read through and thought about the different ways in which the Brit is expressed in the Torah, take a moment to try to outline what responsibilities God and B'nei Yisrael have to each other under its terms:

Activity: Comparing Covenants III

GOD	B'nei Yisrael

A Brit For Today

In many ways the terms of the Brit, and the way it is presented, made a lot of sense thousands of years ago. For example, the promises of success in grain, wine, and oil in *D'varim* chapter 11 (Text 9) matched three industries that were the economic backbone for many villages in ancient Israel. In addition, God's focus on worship fit well in a time when B'nei Yisrael were constantly being tempted by other religions.

Of course, life today is different. In the modern State of Israel, the economy depends on technology and tourism before farming. Internal Jewish issues are more of a concern to the overall religion than Jews leaving B'nei Yisrael behind for another path.

Activity: Renegotiating Terms

Imagine that you have been given a once-in-a-lifetime opportunity – God has invited you, as God's attorney, to re-negotiate the terms of the Brit in light of current events and modern Jewish life. In the space below, fill in what you think makes the most sense for each section of the covenant:

On this date, in the year 20___, The Jewish People make the following Brit with Adonai, our God:

 SECTION I - We the Jewish People agree to do all of the following:

SECTION II - In return, Adonai, our God, agrees to fashion the following rewards:

 SECTION III – If the Jewish People "stray from the path," and neglect to fulfill the responsibilities outlined in SECTION I, God will respond with the following punishments:

Because of our Sins...

As you have seen from studying and discussing the Brit, there is a direct connection in the Torah between the Jewish people keeping God's Mitzvot and our ability to remain and be successful in Eretz Yisrael.

So far, all the texts we have studied have spoken about the future in IF/THEN terms. For example, from *Shmot* chapter 20 – IF you honor your parents, THEN "your days will be long on the land"; from chapter 11 *of D'varim* – IF you follow other gods, THEN God will cause the skies to dry up.

After studying the initial Brit between God and Avraham (Text 4) you were asked to list some examples of "covenants" from your own life. Look again at that list. Choose one of the "covenants" you listed, and answer the following questions about it:

Do both you and the other person/people involved in the covenant have responsibilities, or is it one-sided?

If someone violates the covenant, what happens to that person?

Have you ever broken that covenant? Did the consequences happen or not?

Before we look at how God enforces the circumstances when B'nei Yisrael violate the Brit , what responsibilities do you think God has towards the Jewish people that supersede any Brit enforcement that takes place?

From a reading of the *Tanakh*, (Hebrew Bible) it would seem that God looks at enforcing boundaries and consequences in much the same way that a parent will be enforcing boundaries with their child. Whenever B'nei Yisrael strays from the path – and it happens many times – they temporarily lose their hold on Eretz Yisrael.

B'nei Yisrael finished their journey through the desert and crossed the Jordan River under the leadership of Yehoshu'a. However, God did not exactly present the land to the people on a silver platter. Instead, Eretz Yisrael had to be captured from the nations that were already in the land. Yehoshua's job was to lead the people through this process of taking over the land promised by God to the people.

After the land has been captured, B'nei Yisrael settle in for a long period when there is no real central leadership. Instead, each of the twelve tribes basically keeps to itself, as if the people are part of twelve smaller nations instead of one larger one. Even when threatened by an outside force, it would sometimes take significant pressure for one tribe to come to the defense of another.

For anywhere from 70 to 150 years after the land was captured, B'nei Yisrael were led by wartime leaders known as *Shofetim,* judges. According to the text, these judges were appointed by God to lead B'nei Yisrael in defense of their land, or to recapture the land from temporary victories by their enemies.

The book of *Shofetim* is the first look at how God follows the consequences that were outlined in the Brit back in *D'varim*:

TEXT 10

ה וּבְנֵי יִשְׂרָאֵל, יָשְׁבוּ בְּקֶרֶב הַכְּנַעֲנִי, הַחִתִּי וְהָאֱמֹרִי וְהַפְּרִזִּי, וְהַחִוִּי וְהַיְבוּסִי

5 The Israelites settled among the Canaanites, Hittites, Amorites, Perizzites, Hivites, and Jebusites;

ו וַיִּקְחוּ אֶת-בְּנוֹתֵיהֶם לָהֶם לְנָשִׁים, וְאֶת-בְּנוֹתֵיהֶם נָתְנוּ לִבְנֵיהֶם; וַיַּעַבְדוּ, אֶת-אֱלֹהֵיהֶם.

6 they took their daughters to wife and gave their own daughters to their sons, and they worshiped their gods.

ז וַיַּעֲשׂוּ בְנֵי-יִשְׂרָאֵל אֶת-הָרַע בְּעֵינֵי יְהוָה, וַיִּשְׁכְּחוּ אֶת-יְהוָה אֱלֹהֵיהֶם; וַיַּעַבְדוּ אֶת-הַבְּעָלִים, וְאֶת-הָאֲשֵׁרוֹת

7 The Israelites did what was offensive to *Adonai*; they ignored *Adonai* their God and worshiped the *Baalim* and the *Asheroth*.

ח וַיִּחַר-אַף יְהוָה, בְּיִשְׂרָאֵל, וַיִּמְכְּרֵם בְּיַד כּוּשַׁן רִשְׁעָתַיִם, מֶלֶךְ אֲרַם נַהֲרָיִם; וַיַּעַבְדוּ בְנֵי-יִשְׂרָאֵל אֶת-כּוּשַׁן רִשְׁעָתַיִם, שְׁמֹנֶה שָׁנִים

8 The LORD became incensed at Israel and surrendered them to King *Cushan-rishathaim* of *Aram-naharaim*; and the Israelites were subject to *Cushan-rishathaim* for eight years.

ט וַיִּזְעֲקוּ בְנֵי-יִשְׂרָאֵל אֶל-יְהוָה, וַיָּקֶם יְהוָה מוֹשִׁיעַ לִבְנֵי יִשְׂרָאֵל וַיּוֹשִׁיעֵם--אֵת עָתְנִיאֵל בֶּן-קְנַז, אֲחִי כָלֵב הַקָּטֹן מִמֶּנּוּ

9 The Israelites cried out to *Adonai*, and *Adonai* raised a champion for the Israelites to deliver them: Othniel the Kenizzite, a younger kinsman of Caleb.

י וַתְּהִי עָלָיו רוּחַ-יְהוָה, וַיִּשְׁפֹּט אֶת-יִשְׂרָאֵל, וַיֵּצֵא לַמִּלְחָמָה, וַיִּתֵּן יְהוָה בְּיָדוֹ אֶת-כּוּשַׁן רִשְׁעָתַיִם מֶלֶךְ אֲרָם; וַתָּעָז יָדוֹ, עַל כּוּשַׁן רִשְׁעָתָיִם

10 The spirit of *Adonai* descended upon him and he became Israel's chieftain. He went out to war, and *Adonai* delivered King Cushan-rishathaim of Aram into his hands. He prevailed over Cushan-rishathaim,

יא וַתִּשְׁקֹט הָאָרֶץ, אַרְבָּעִים שָׁנָה; וַיָּמָת, עָתְנִיאֵל בֶּן-קְנַז.

11 and the land had peace for forty years. Then Othniel the Kenizzite died...

שופטים ג:ה-י"א   *Shofetim chapter 3, verses 5-11*

After everything *Adonai* has done for B'nei Yisrael –freeing them from Egypt, helping them to capture Eretz Yisrael— why do you think they are so quick to worship other gods? Why is it so easy to forget that the Brit has consequences for violations on the part of B'nei Yisrael?

Once again, B'nei Yisrael have to "cry out" before they are rescued by God. What form do you think this "crying out" took? Why does God wait for B'nei Yisrael to cry out before rescuing them?

It is clear from this and other texts that all the people in B'nei Yisrael are treated like one "party" in the Brit— a Jew who is following God's will is swept away along with those who are violating it. Do you think this is fair? Can you think of any alternatives that work but still fulfill the terms of the Brit?

Have you ever been in a situation where you experienced a negative consequence for the actions of others? Can you think of any examples in which the concept of group consequences makes sense?

After the time of the Judges, in about 1050 BCE, the tribes of B'nei Yisrael became united for the first time under one government, with King Sha'ul at the head. After Sha'ul, King David continued to unite the people, and for the first time established Jerusalem as the physical capital for Eretz Yisrael and the spiritual center for B'nei Yisrael. Jerusalem reaches its first height under David's son, Shlomo, who builds God's Temple in Jerusalem when he becomes King.

Unfortunately, the unity did not last. After his death Sh'lomo's sons fought over who would rule B'nei Yisrael and ended up splitting the kingdom. The ten northern tribes became the kingdom of Israel, and the remaining southern tribes ruled from Jerusalem over the kingdom of Judea.

Yirmiyahu was the prophet for the King of Judea when the first Temple in Jerusalem was destroyed by the Babylonian king Nebuchadnezzar in 586 BCE. While the following prophesy was delivered decades before the attack, it gives a good idea of the kind of statements from God the prophet Yirmiyahu was asked to deliver. That this prophesy was focused on something years into the future also gives us a good idea of how many chances God was willing to give B'nei Yisrael before resorting to consequences.

TEXT 11

ב כֹּה אָמַר יְהוָה
זָכַרְתִּי לָךְ חֶסֶד נְעוּרַיִךְ, אַהֲבַת כְּלוּלֹתָיִךְ—
לֶכְתֵּךְ אַחֲרַי בַּמִּדְבָּר, בְּאֶרֶץ לֹא זְרוּעָה

2 ...Thus said *Adonai*:
"I accounted to your favor The devotion of your youth, Your love as a bride -- How you followed Me in the wilderness, In a land not sown.

ג קֹדֶשׁ יִשְׂרָאֵל לַיהוָה, רֵאשִׁית תְּבוּאָתֹה;
כָּל-אֹכְלָיו יֶאְשָׁמוּ, רָעָה תָּבֹא אֲלֵיהֶם נְאֻם-
יְהוָה.

3 Israel was holy to *Adonai*, The first fruits of God's harvest. All who ate of it [by attacking the people of Israel] were held guilty; Disaster befell them" -- declares *Adonai*.

These first two verses reflect God's special relationship with B'nei Yisrael.
Why do you think God chooses to open what is a negative prophesy with such clear statements of the love that exists between *Adonai* and B'nei Yisrael?

ד שִׁמְעוּ דְבַר-יְהֹוָה, בֵּית יַעֲקֹב, וְכָל-מִשְׁפְּחוֹת, בֵּית יִשְׂרָאֵל

4 Hear the word of *Adonai*, O House of Jacob, Every clan of the House of Israel!

ה כֹּה אָמַר יְהֹוָה, מַה-מָּצְאוּ אֲבוֹתֵיכֶם בִּי עָוֶל--כִּי רָחֲקוּ, מֵעָלָי; וַיֵּלְכוּ אַחֲרֵי הַהֶבֶל, וַיֶּהְבָּלוּ

5 Thus said *Adonai*:
"What wrong did your fathers find in Me That they abandoned Me And went after delusion and were deluded?

ו וְלֹא אָמְרוּ
אַיֵּה יְהֹוָה, הַמַּעֲלֶה אֹתָנוּ מֵאֶרֶץ מִצְרָיִם; הַמּוֹלִיךְ אֹתָנוּ בַּמִּדְבָּר, בְּאֶרֶץ עֲרָבָה וְשׁוּחָה בְּאֶרֶץ צִיָּה וְצַלְמָוֶת--בְּאֶרֶץ לֹא-עָבַר בָּהּ אִישׁ, וְלֹא-יָשַׁב אָדָם שָׁם

6 They never asked themselves:
'Where is *Adonai*, Who brought us up from the land of Egypt, Who led us through the wilderness, A land of deserts and pits, A land of drought and darkness, A land no man had traversed, Where no human being had dwelt?'

ז וָאָבִיא אֶתְכֶם אֶל-אֶרֶץ הַכַּרְמֶל, לֶאֱכֹל פִּרְיָהּ וְטוּבָהּ; וַתָּבֹאוּ וַתְּטַמְּאוּ אֶת-אַרְצִי, וְנַחֲלָתִי שַׂמְתֶּם לְתוֹעֵבָה

7 I brought you to this country of farm land, to enjoy its fruit and its bounty; But you came and defiled My land, You made My possession abhorrent.

ח הַכֹּהֲנִים, לֹא אָמְרוּ אַיֵּה יְהֹוָה, וְתֹפְשֵׂי הַתּוֹרָה לֹא יְדָעוּנִי, וְהָרֹעִים פָּשְׁעוּ בִי; וְהַנְּבִיאִים נִבְּאוּ בַבַּעַל, וְאַחֲרֵי לֹא-יוֹעִלוּ הָלָכוּ

8 The priests never asked themselves:
'Where is *Adonai*?'
The guardians of the Teaching ignored Me; The rulers rebelled against Me, And the prophets prophesied by Baal [a rival god] And followed what can do no good.

ט לָכֵן, עֹד אָרִיב אִתְּכֶם--נְאֻם-יְהֹוָה; וְאֶת-בְּנֵי בְנֵיכֶם, אָרִיב

9 Oh, I will go on arguing against you" – declares *Adonai* – "And I will argue against your children's children!

יא הַהֵימִיר גּוֹי אֱלֹהִים, וְהֵמָּה לֹא אֱלֹהִים; וְעַמִּי הֵמִיר כְּבוֹדוֹ, בְּלוֹא יוֹעִיל

11 Has any nation changed its gods Even though they are [not even real] gods? But My people has exchanged its glory For what can do no good.

יב שֹׁמּוּ שָׁמַיִם, עַל-זֹאת; וְשַׂעֲרוּ חָרְבוּ מְאֹד, נְאֻם-יְהֹוָה

12 Be appalled, O heavens, at this; Be horrified, utterly dazed!" – says *Adonai*.

יג כִּי-שְׁתַּיִם רָעוֹת, עָשָׂה עַמִּי: אֹתִי עָזְבוּ מְקוֹר מַיִם חַיִּים, לַחְצֹב לָהֶם בֹּארוֹת--בֹּארֹת נִשְׁבָּרִים, אֲשֶׁר לֹא-יָכִלוּ הַמָּיִם

13 "For My people have done a twofold wrong: They have forsaken Me, the Fount of living waters, And hewed cisterns✿ for themselves, broken cisterns, Which cannot even hold water.

יד הַעֶבֶד, יִשְׂרָאֵל--אִם-יְלִיד בַּיִת, הוּא: מַדּוּעַ, הָיָה לָבַז

14 Is Israel a bondman? Is he a home-born slave? Then why is he given over to plunder?

טו עָלָיו יִשְׁאֲגוּ כְפִרִים, נָתְנוּ קוֹלָם; וַיָּשִׁיתוּ אַרְצוֹ לְשַׁמָּה, עָרָיו נצתה (נִצְּתוּ) מִבְּלִי יֹשֵׁב

15 Lions have roared over him, Have raised their cries. They have made his land a waste, His cities desolate, without inhabitants.

ירמיהו ב:ב-ט, י"א-ט"ו   *Yirmiyahu* chapter 2, verses 2-9, 11-15

✿A cistern (here used as a metaphor for idols) is an underground reservoir where water from the rainy season can keep all year.

What have B'nei Yisrael done to violate the Brit?

Most of this message from God does not focus on what B'nei Yisrael have technically done wrong. Think of a close relationship as you read God's words in verses 5-12. If you could connect human emotions to God, how does God feel as a result of the behaviors of B'nei Yisrael?

There is a large amount of imagery and metaphor used in this text. For example, in verse 13, instead of saying that B'nei Yisrael have started crafting and worshipping idols, God speaks of them digging "broken cisterns, which cannot hold water." Why do you think God's prophet, Yirmiyahu, speaks in this way?

What parallels, if any, can you find between this text and D'varim chapter 11 (Text 9)? Are God's emotions portrayed in the same way, or differently in these two texts?

Look at the last two verses. According to this prophesy, looking into the future, how has God fulfilled the consequences outlined in the Brit?

Yirmiyahu's prophesy above is just one of many texts in the Tanakh that confirm the terms of the Brit time after time. There is a consistency to what God expects of B'nei Yisrael and what the results will be if we do not deliver.

So what does God expect of B'nei Yisrael? According to what we have looked at so far, God seems most concerned with worship. In a world in which B'nei Yisrael are surrounded and constantly tempted by alternate gods to Adonai, it is abandoning Adonai for these other gods that makes God the most angry.

Exile and Redemption

Any significant period during which B'nei Yisrael are kept out of Eretz Yisrael by force is known as a Galut, or Exile. For example, even though they had not yet become the rulers of Eretz Yisrael, the 400 years spent in Egyptian slavery are considered to be the first Galut, in Jewish tradition. The two most difficult Exiles, however, were the ones that followed the destruction of the two Temples in Jerusalem.

In 586 BCE, when the Babylonian king Nebuchadnezzar destroyed the Temple and exiled B'nei Yisrael from the land, it could have destroyed the Jewish people. A nation that was accustomed to worshipping Adonai primarily through animal sacrifice and Temple-based rituals suddenly had to find a way to connect to God without God's house being intact. A people who had experienced hundreds of years and generation after generation of home rule were suddenly thrust into an alien environment, far from the land they loved.

While B'nei Yisrael eventually thrived in this strange land, they had no way of knowing if they would ever get the chance to return.

B'nei Yisrael eventually got the chance to return to Eretz Yisrael and rebuild the Temple. This was done thanks to the Persian emperor, Cyrus the Great. Cyrus believed in Jewish prophesies that predicted a return to Eretz Yisrael, and decided to help fulfill those prophesies by sending anyone who wanted to go back to Israel from Babylonia, with a decree that they should build a new Temple in Jerusalem. This Second Temple was completed around 516 BCE, only 70 years after the previous one was destroyed. While B'nei Yisrael were no longer fully in charge of the government in Eretz Yisrael since they were part of the Persian empire, there was real optimism again among the people now that they had returned to the land.

When B'nei Yisrael have been in Galut and are given the opportunity to return to Eretz Yisrael it is known as Ge'ulah (redemption).

During the time of the Second Temple, Eretz Yisrael changed hands multiple times, eventually ending up as part of the Roman empire. While life under the Romans started out good, with a virtually free Jewish monarchy ruling over the land, it became harsher and more restrictive as time went on. By the time a portion of the Jewish population began to revolt against the Romans in 66 CE, Roman rule had become oppressive, regularly attempting to stifle the Jewish religion and replace it with Roman beliefs and values. Four years into the revolt, on the Ninth of Av (August 4) in 70 CE, the Second Temple was destroyed. The largest Galut and the longest so far in Jewish history, began with the destruction of the Temple. Many Jews even say that, as long

The Land that was Lost

It is easy to get absorbed in the theological, historical and political details of how we ended up in the Galut, and in the challenges we faced once we spread out around the world. To only focus on those areas is to leave out one important idea - the special place the land itself has in the hearts of B'nei Yisrael. It is very clear from our texts that Erertz Yisrael is not just a land to live in - it is also meant to be a land to enjoy, a land that can inspire all who gaze upon it.

TEXT 12

הַיּוֹם, אַתֶּם יֹצְאִים, בְּחֹדֶשׁ, הָאָבִיב - ד

4 Today, in the month of Spring, you are exiting (Egypt).

וְהָיָה כִי-יְבִיאֲךָ יְהוָה אֶל- ה
אֶרֶץ הַכְּנַעֲנִי וְהַחִתִּי וְהָאֱמֹרִי וְהַחִוִּי וְהַיְבוּ
סִי, אֲשֶׁר נִשְׁבַּע לַאֲבֹתֶיךָ לָתֶת לָךְ, אֶרֶץ זָב
ת חָלָב, וּדְבָשׁ; וְעָבַדְתָּ אֶת-
הָעֲבֹדָה הַזֹּאת, בַּחֹדֶשׁ הַזֶּה

5 And it will come to pass, when Adonai brings you to the land of the K'na'ani, Hiti, Emori, Hivi, and Yevusi; [the land] that [God] promised your ancestors would be given to you, a land flowing with milk and honey; you will perform this service or worship, in this month.

שמות י״ג: ד-ה   Shmot Chapter 13, Verses 4-5

ו וְשָׁמַרְתָּ, אֶת-מִצְוֹת יְהוָה אֱלֹהֶיךָ, לָלֶכֶת בִּדְרָכָיו, וּלְיִרְאָה אֹתוֹ

6 And you will observe the commandments of Adonai your God, to walk in God's path, and to be in awe of God.

ז כִּי יְהוָה אֱלֹהֶיךָ, מְבִיאֲךָ אֶל-אֶרֶץ טוֹבָה : אֶרֶץ, נַחֲלֵי מָיִם--עֲיָנֹת וּתְהֹמֹת, יֹצְאִים בַּבִּקְעָה וּבָהָר

7 for Adonai, your God, has brought you to a good land; a land of streams full of water - springs and great depths, exiting in the plains and in the mountains.

ח אֶרֶץ חִטָּה וּשְׂעֹרָה, וְגֶפֶן וּתְאֵנָה וְרִמּוֹן ; אֶרֶץ-זֵית שֶׁמֶן, וּדְבָשׁ

8 A land of wheat and barley, [grape] vines and figs and pomegranates; a land of olive oil and honey.

ט אֶרֶץ, אֲשֶׁר לֹא בְמִסְכֵּנֻת תֹּאכַל-בָּהּ לֶחֶם--לֹא-תֶחְסַר כֹּל, בָּהּ ; אֶרֶץ אֲשֶׁר אֲבָנֶיהָ בַרְזֶל, וּמֵהֲרָרֶיהָ תַּחְצֹב נְחֹשֶׁת

9 A land in which one does not eat bread while in danger -- where nothing is missing for anyone who lives there; a land in which its stones are iron, and in which copper is mined in its mountains.

י וְאָכַלְתָּ, וְשָׂבָעְתָּ--וּבֵרַכְתָּ אֶת-יְהוָה אֱלֹהֶיךָ, עַל-הָאָרֶץ הַטֹּבָה אֲשֶׁר נָתַן-לָךְ

10 And you will eat, be satisfied, and then bless Adonai, your God for the good land that was given to you.

דברים ח : ו-י   *D'varim* Chapter 8, Verses 6-10

When the people of Israel are first exiting Egypt, and later while they are wandering in the desert, God tells them all about the land that they are traveling to.

Make a list of what God has emphasized in these texts from Shmot and D'varim. Can you find anything that the items on the list have in common?

_____

_____

_____

_____

When we talk about the Land of Israel today we tend to talk about the simple beauty of the desert, or the amazement one has when watching the sun rise over the Dead Sea - things that speak to the natural beauty of the Land. Why do you think God puts an emphasis on the items in the list you just made? What might this tell us about what God thinks the priorities of the people will be once they have settled the land?

וְעַלוּ אֶל אָבִי
אֶרֶץ יִשְׂרָאֵל גָּבוֹהַ מִכָּל הָאֲרָצוֹת

And go up to my father
The land of Israel is higher than all other lands

רש"י שמות מ"ה: ט   Rashi on *Shmot* Chapter 45, Verse 9

The concept expressed in this piece from Rashi is still in practice today. The act of moving to Israel is called "Aliyah," which means going up. Keep in mind that the Torah never states outright that the Land of Israel is on a higher level than other lands - we get this idea from those who help us to understand the words of the Torah such as Rashi.

The world is full of places that can be meaningful to visit. Do you agree with this tradition that the Land of Israel is automatically higher than other lands? Why do you think such an idea has been so important to us over the last 2,000 years?

TEXT 15

כשעלה ר׳ חנינא הגדול מבבל
בקש לידע אם נכנס לא״יי והיה שוקל
אבנים
כל זמן שהיו קלות אמר עדיין לא נכנסתי
לארץ ישראל
כיון שמצאן כבידות אמר אין אלו אלא
אבני ארץ ישראל והיה מנשקן

When Rabbi Hanina the Great ascended [to the Land of Israel] from Babylon
he had to figure out when he had arrived in the land.
He weighed the stones [along the way].
As long as the stones were light, he said "I have still not arrived in the land."
However, when he found that the stones were getting heavier, he said "these can be no other stones but the stones of Israel!"
[in his great joy] he kissed the stones [of the Land of Israel].

תוספות, כתובות דף קי״ב עמוד א   Tosfot on Ketubot page 112, side A

One interesting part of this text is that Rabbi Hanina kisses the stones of the Land when he arrives. This is one of the earliest examples of what many people do today when they arrive in Israel for the first time, which is to kiss the ground the first time they set foot on it.

What is this story trying to tell us about the Land when it tells us that the stones in Israel are somehow heavier than they are in other places? Do you think there is a relationship between this text and Rashi talking about Israel being "higher" than other lands?

The next text involves a foreign King trying to convince the Jewish People to leave the Land of Israel and travel to his land instead:

TEXT 16

אַל-תִּשְׁמְעוּ, אֶל- לֹא
חִזְקִיָּהוּ: כִּי כֹה אָמַר מֶלֶךְ-אַשּׁוּר, עֲשׂוּ-
אִתִּי בְרָכָה וּצְאוּ אֵלַי, וְאִכְלוּ-אִישׁ-
גַּפְנוֹ וְאִישׁ תְּאֵנָתוֹ, וּשְׁתוּ אִישׁ מֵי-בֹרוֹ

31 "Don't listen to Hizkiyahu! For thus says the King of Ashur: 'do me a blessing (favor) and come out to me, and a person can eat form the land's vines and figs, and drink from the water of the land's pits.

עַד-בֹּאִי וְלָקַחְתִּי אֶתְכֶם אֶל-
אֶרֶץ כְּאַרְצְכֶם, אֶרֶץ דָּגָן וְתִירוֹשׁ אֶרֶץ לֶחֶם
וּכְרָמִים אֶרֶץ זֵית יִצְהָר וּדְבַשׁ, וִחְיוּ, וְלֹא תָ
מֻתוּ

32 Until I come and bring you to a land like your land, a land of grains and wine, a land full of bread and vineyards, a land of olive oil and honey, and you will live there, and not die.

מלכים ב י״ח: ל״א-ל״ב   Kings 2, Chapter 18, Verses 31-32

Do you see a parallel between what the King of Ashur is using to entice the people and some of the other texts we have studied?

What does the King of Ashur think that B'nei Yisrael are looking for in a homeland?

An early proposal for the Jewish State involved placing it in a different part of the world - for example, in Africa. The King of Ashur here is promising something very similar.

What do you think of the idea of setting up the Jewish homeland somewhere different from the Land of Israel?

TEXT 17

נוֹדֶה לְךָ ה' אֱלֹהֵינוּ
עַל שֶׁהִנְחַלְתָּ לַאֲבוֹתֵינוּ
אֶרֶץ חֶמְדָּה טוֹבָה וּרְחָבָה

We are thankful to you, Adonai our God, that you bestowed a delightful, good, and broad land to our ancestors...

ברכת המזון   Birkat HaMazon

In multiple places in Jewish text, such as in this paragraph from Birkat HaMazon, we are told that the Land is "good."

What is your definition of a good land? Do you think your definition matches the definition of a "good" land that appears in Birkat HaMazon?

There have been many different responses over the years to how we came to be in a state of Galut and how we can achieve Geulah. Even though we have looked in detail at the Brit, it is important to understand how the Rabbis, suddenly the leaders of the Jewish community worldwide, explained what led to the Galut, and how to react to it:

TEXT 18

מקדש ראשון מפני מה חרב? מפני שלשה
דברים שהיו בו : עבודה זרה, וגלוי
עריות,ושפיכות דמים

Why was the first Temple destroyed?
Because of three things that took place in the people: idol worship, immoral sexual practices, and the spilling of blood (murder).

אבל מקדש שני, שהיו עוסקין בתורה
ובמצות וגמילות חסדים מפני מה
חרב? מפני שהיתה בו שנאת חנם

But in the time of the second Temple, when [the people] were busy with Torah, Mitzvot, and acts of kindness, why was it destroyed? Because there was senseless hatred of one another.

ללמדך ששקולה שנאת חנם כנגד שלש
עבירות: עבודה זרה, גלוי עריות, ושפיכות
דמים

This is to teach us that senseless hatred weighs as heavily as the other three transgressions.

מסכת יומא דף ט עמוד ב   Talmud Yoma, page 9 side B

מִשֶּׁחָרַב בֵּית הַמִּקְדָּשׁ, תִּקְנוּ חֲכָמִים שֶׁהָיוּ בְּאוֹתוֹ הַדּוֹר

Because of the destruction of the Temple, the sages legislated that in that generation:

שֶׁהָעוֹרֵךְ שֻׁלְחָן לַעֲשׂוֹת סְעוֹדָה לָאוֹרְחִים,מְחַסֵּר מִמֶּנּוּ מְעַט, וּמַנִּיחַ מָקוֹם פָּנוּי, בְּלֹא קְעָרָה מִן הַקְּעָרוֹת הָרְאוּיוֹת לָתֵת שָׁם

A person hosting guests for a banquet should give a little less food, and also leave an open seat, without the same dish as the kind everyone else has in front of themselves...

וּכְשֶׁהֶחָתָן נוֹשֵׂא, לוֹקֵחַ אֵפֶר מִקְלֶה וְנוֹתֵן בְּרֹאשׁוֹ מְקוֹם הֲנָחַת תְּפִלִּין

When a groom gets married, he should take some light dust and place it on his head, where the Tefillin normally go...

וְכֵן גָּזְרוּ שֶׁלֹּא לְנַגֵּן בִּכְלֵי שִׁיר, כֻּלָּם ; וְכָל מִינֵי זֶמֶר, וְכָל מַשְׁמִיעֵי קוֹל שֶׁלְּשִׁיר--אָסוּר לִשְׂמֹחַ בָּהֶן, וְאָסוּר לְשָׁמְעָן : מִפְּנֵי הֶחָרְבָּן. וַאֲפִלּוּ שִׁירָה בַּפֶּה עַל הַיַּיִן--אֲסוּרָה

They also decreed that it is forbidden to play happy music on any instrument; that every type of song, and every noise that is for singing happy songs is also forbidden. Even singing vocally over the wine - forbidden.

רמב"ם הלכות תעניות פרק ה

Rambam laws of Fasts, chapter 5 (selections)

Why do you think the rabbis focus on Jerusalem's destruction more deeply than on the exile from the rest of the land? (this question can be answered from many perspectives: religious, political, geographical, historical...)

How do you feel about the various rules that were established after the destruction of the Second Temple?

Do you think these laws were an appropriate way to mourn the destruction of Jerusalem?

Activity - Marketing Israel

You are God's marketing director. Your job is to sell the idea of the Land of Israel to B'nei Yisrael. Remember, they have been slaves for hundreds of years and have trouble trusting the word of God who none of them have ever experienced.

Using the texts that were in this section, design part of an ad campaign (poster, email, TV ad script) that will get B'nei Yisrael excited for their eventual arrival in the promised land.

Loss of Jerusalem = Exile

While the concept of a Galut is generally about our exile from Eretz Yisrael as a whole, there is a special place reserved in the hearts of B'nei Yisrael for Jerusalem, and the Temples that once stood in the city. There are a number of reasons why Jerusalem figures so centrally into the despair at our loss of the land as a whole:

- While Eretz Yisrael in its entirety is special for the Jewish people, it is Jerusalem - and only Jerusalem - that was singled out by God to be the center of worship for B'nei Yisrael. It is made very clear in the Torah and other texts that offerings can only take place at God's designated place - which eventually comes to mean Jerusalem.

- It is important to remember that at the time the first Temple was destroyed B'nei Yisrael only knew one method to communicate something directly to God - making an offering at the altar in Jerusalem. Whether someone needed to repent, make a request, or just say "thanks" to *Adonai*, it was achieved through an offering. The structure and contents of *Tefillah*, Jewish Prayer, were originally considered to be a temporary replacement for offerings and not a permanent form of communication with God.

- Out of the 613 *Mitzvot*, commands, in the Torah, 1 out of every 6 is related to offerings, with dozens more focused on rituals that can only take place when there is an altar (and therefore a Temple) in Jerusalem. The loss of the Temple suddenly cut the people off from one of the key ways in which B'nei Yisrael fulfilled God's will.

- As we noted, during their first few generations in the Land B'nei Yisrael often behaved like 12 separate nations instead of one unified one. It was King David who unified B'nei Yisrael for the first time and made Jerusalem his seat of power. From when King David first captured the city about 3000 years ago Jerusalem has been the symbol of Jewish rule in Eretz Yisrael. To a certain extent the loss of Jerusalem is also mourned as a loss of Jewish unity.

Living In The West

Both the Tanakh and the rabbis had very clear ideas on what it meant to live in Exile from the land of Israel.

TEXT 20

טז לָכֵן אֱמֹר, כֹּה-אָמַר אֲדֹ-נָי ה', כִּי הִרְחַקְתִּים בַּגּוֹיִם, וְכִי הֲפִיצוֹתִים בָּאֲרָצוֹת; וָאֱהִי לָהֶם לְמִקְדָּשׁ מְעַט, בָּאֲרָצוֹת אֲשֶׁר-בָּאוּ שָׁם.

16 therefore say: The Lord God said: Although I have removed them far off among the nations, and although I have scattered them among the countries, yet have I been to them as a little sanctuary in the countries where they are come;

יז לָכֵן אֱמֹר, כֹּה-אָמַר אֲדֹ-נָי ה', וְקִבַּצְתִּי אֶתְכֶם מִן-הָעַמִּים, וְאָסַפְתִּי אֶתְכֶם מִן-הָאֲרָצוֹת אֲשֶׁר נְפֹצוֹתֶם בָּהֶם; וְנָתַתִּי לָכֶם, אֶת-אַדְמַת יִשְׂרָאֵל.

17 therefore say: The Lord God Said: I will even gather you from the peoples, and assemble you out of the countries where ye have been scattered, and I will give you the land of Israel.

יט וְנָתַתִּי לָהֶם לֵב אֶחָד, וְרוּחַ חֲדָשָׁה אֶתֵּן בְּקִרְבְּכֶם; וַהֲסִרֹתִי לֵב הָאֶבֶן, מִבְּשָׂרָם, וְנָתַתִּי לָהֶם, לֵב בָּשָׂר.

19 And I will give them one heart, and I will put a new spirit within you; and I will remove the stony heart out of their flesh, and will give them a heart of flesh;

כ לְמַעַן בְּחֻקֹּתַי יֵלֵכוּ, וְאֶת-מִשְׁפָּטַי יִשְׁמְרוּ וְעָשׂוּ אֹתָם; וְהָיוּ-לִי לְעָם--וַאֲנִי, אֶהְיֶה לָהֶם לֵאלֹקִים.

20 that they may walk in My statutes, and keep Mine ordinances, and do them; and they shall be My people, and I will be their God.

יחזקל י״א : טז-י״ז, י״ט-כ   *Yehezkel* chapter 11, verses 16-17 and 19-20

What do you think the text means when it states that God has been a "little sanctuary" for the people while in exile?

What aspects of living spread out among the nations might necessitate a "little sanctuary" provided by God?

TEXT 21

אמר רב ענן כל הקבור בארץ ישראל כאילו קבור תחת המזבח כתיב הכא (שמות כ) מזבח אדמה תעשה לי וכתיב התם (דברים לב) וכפר אדמתו עמו

R. Anan said; Whoever is buried in the Land of Israel is deemed to be buried under the altar; since in respect of the latter it is written in Scripture, *At altar of earth you shall make unto me,* and in respect of the former it is written in Scripture, *And his laud doth make expiation for his people.*

כתובות דף קי״א עמוד א   *Ketubot* Page 111, side A

This statement is related to the belief that as part of the time of Mashiach the dead will be resurrected in some form.

Do you think this opinion is connected to the earlier texts we looked at that talked about the Land of Israel being more special than other lands? Why or why not?

Rabbi Eleazar's message in this text is very clear - if you want to be part of the resurrection, make sure you die in the Land of Israel. Think about that for a second though - in his time travel to Israel was more expensive, and absolutely more dangerous, than it is today.

Do you think it is fair to penalize those who do not have the means to travel to the Land? Why or why not?

TEXT 22 – SELECTIONS FROM RAMBAM* LAWS OF KINGS, CHAPTER 5: LAW 11 (*Rabbi Moses ben Maimon—Maimonides)

אָסוּר לָצֵאת מֵאֶרֶץ יִשְׂרָאֵל לְחוּצָה לָאָרֶץ לְעוֹלָם—אֶלָּא
לִלְמֹד תּוֹרָה
אוֹ לִשָּׂא אִשָּׁה
אוֹ לְהַצִּיל מִיַּד הַגּוֹיִים
וְיַחֲזֹר לָאָרֶץ ; וְכֵן יוֹצֵא הוּא לִסְחוֹרָה

It is always forbidden to leave the Land of Israel (once you have moved there) except for the following situations:
- To study Torah
- To get married
- To escape from other nations
After any of the above is settled, one must return to the land.
This also applies to doing business.

Do you think these laws are harsh on people who move out of Israel, or who never move there in the first place? Why or why not?

Why do you think Rambam chooses these four reasons that it is OK to leave the land? Do you think he would want these to be interpreted broadly or narrowly?

According to Rambam, if one of his four reasons did take someone out of the Land of Israel, how long would it be acceptable to wait before returning?

Today a family will sometimes go on Aliyah and then find that they can not make a living in Israel; Often such a family has no option but to return to where they came from.

Do you think Rambam would consider this leaving Israel for "doing business?"

LAW 15

לְעוֹלָם יָדוּר אָדָם בְּאֶרֶץ יִשְׂרָאֵל, אֲפִלּוּ בְּעִיר שֶׁרֻבָּהּ גּוֹיִים
וְאַל יָדוּר בְּחוּצָה לָאָרֶץ, וַאֲפִלּוּ בְּעִיר שֶׁרֻבָּהּ יִשְׂרָאֵל
שֶׁכָּל הַיּוֹצֵא לְחוּצָה לָאָרֶץ--כְּאִלּוּ עוֹבֵד עֲבוֹדָה זָרָה

A person should always dwell in Israel, even in a non-Jewish town.
A person should never live outside of Israel, even in a Jewish town.
For anyone who lives outside of the Land, it is as if he is an idol worshipper...

We know from much of Rambam's writings that he was very concerned about assimilation by the Jews of Northern Africa and Spain; the form of Islam practiced in many of these countries, some with large Jewish population centers, was very enticing.

Knowing these details about Rambam's world, do you think his judgments about different towns in Law 15 are fair or not?

While Rambam seems to have very strong negative opinions about any choice to live outside of Israel, there is an interesting statement he makes at the end of this section:

כְּשֵׁם שֶׁאָסוּר לָצֵאת מֵהָאָרֶץ לְחוּצָה לָאָרֶץ--כָּךְ אָסוּר לָצֵאת מִבָּבֶל לִשְׁאָר אֲרָצוֹת

Just like it is forbidden to leave Israel for living outside of Israel -- It is also forbidden to leave Babylonia for other lands...

Babylonia was the center of Jewish thought and Jewish life in exile for nearly 1000 years. Most of the Judaism that we observe today was developed at the Yeshivot in its cities of Sura and Pumpeditha. This law was not even created by Rambam - instead, he is quoting from the rabbis own thoughts while developing the laws in the Babylonian exile.

While Laws 11 and 15 seem to condemn those who move from or just live outside of Israel, Law 16 makes us pause and think.

Why might it be alright to live in the Jewish society in Babylonia as opposed to living in other lands?

One possibility to consider is that Rambam and the rabbis of the Talmud are giving recognition that it is possible to create a Jewish center of life outside of the land of Israel. Remember that the rabbis who first wrote this law were themselves descendants of Jews who were given the option of returning to the Land in the time of Cyrus - but chose the comfort and stability of Babylonia instead.

What we have in the words of the Talmud as conveyed by Rambam is the possibility of dual loyalty - loyalty to the Jewish community in one's home country at the same time as having loyalty to the Land of Israel.

Most of us studying this book will never move to Israel. We might spend a summer there, or even a year there, but very few of us will make it our permanent home. When we point this out, a question emerges:

How do we maintain a relationship with Israel - both the State and the Land - while living outside the Land in North America?

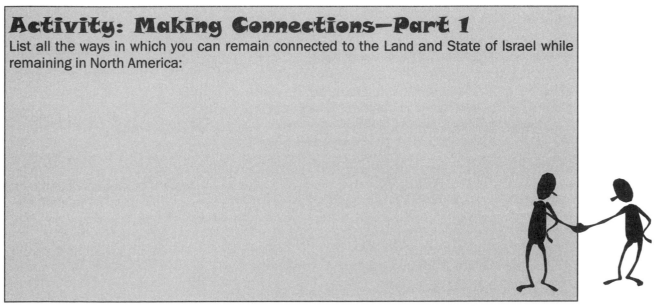

Activity: Making Connections—Part 1
List all the ways in which you can remain connected to the Land and State of Israel while remaining in North America:

Activity: Making Connections: Part 2

How many connections did you list on the previous page? How many can you add?

In the space before each answer fill in 1, 2, 3, 4 or 5 to indicate how often you would have the opportunity to enhance your connection to Israel.

1 = hourly
2 = daily
3 = weekly
4 = monthly
5 = annually

- ☐ Sing Hatikvah
- ☐ Pray for peace in Israel
- ☐ Read an Israeli newspaper online
- ☐ Read the printed version of an Israeli newspaper
- ☐ Hang an artistic "Mizrach" on the eastern wall of your family room, living room, bedroom, den, etc...
- ☐ Attend a pro-Israel rally or demonstration
- ☐ Write a letter to your national leadership encouraging US or Canadian support of Israel
- ☐ Travel to Israel
- ☐ Speak to an Israeli
- ☐ Watch an Israeli TV show or movie
- ☐ Listen to Israeli music
- ☐ Send care packages to Israeli soldiers
- ☐ Working with others, donate equipment to an Israeli army unit, hospital, or school
- ☐ Debate and discuss Israel issues with your friends
- ☐ Speak in Hebrew
- ☐ Learn a Hebrew word
- ☐ Hang decorations related to Israel - the Israeli flag, a picture of Ben Gurion, a Hebrew poster for your favorite movie - in your room.
- ☐ Sing and dance on Yom HaAtzmaut
- ☐ Have a moment of silence on Yom HaZikaron
- ☐ Participate in an online discussion on Israel
- ☐ Write something about Israel as your Facebook status update, or on a friend's wall
- ☐ Look for news about Israel in your local newspaper
- ☐ Participate in Israeli dancing
- ☐ Sing Israeli folk songs such as Bashana HaBa'ah

Now can you think of any others to add?

Hopes and Prayers

B'nei Yisrael have always had various methods of communicating with God. Our leadership, from *Avraham* all the way to *Moshe*, were able to communicate directly with God, one on one. Many commentators such as *Rambam* believe that *Moshe* had the closest relationship with God in our history. There are two excellent examples of just how personal the give and take between *Moshe* and *Adonai* was.

When B'nei Yisrael are stuck between the Sea and the Egyptian chariots, *Moshe* turns to God with a prayer asking for help. Instead of a comforting reply, or a reminder of the Brit, *Adonai* essentially tells *Moshe* to get up and do something about it - that there is a time for prayer, and a time for action, and this is the latter. (*Shmot* chapter 14 verse 15)

After the failure of the nation during the Golden Calf, God is ready to destroy B'nei Yisrael and just start over again with *Moshe* as the founder of a new people. There is a telling moment during this part of the story that reveals just how comfortable God and *Moshe* seem to be with each other. After hearing the threat from God to destroy B'nei Yisrael, *Moshe* responds with a strong request of his own: "Now, if you will forgive their sin... but if not, erase me, please, from this book you have written." *Moshe's* willingness to stand up to *Adonai*, and God's willingness to hear *Moshe's* requests, is what saves B'nei Yisrael from the worst of God's anger after the calf. (*Shmot* chapter 32 verse 32)

Of course, not everyone can be *Moshe*, and *Moshe* did not have the time or ability to handle every communication with God. Also, as the Golden Calf incident revealed, the people depended so much on *Moshe* as their conduit to God that they had to immediately replace him with another representative to God when he stayed too long on Mt. Sinai. It is no coincidence that the Golden Calf incident occurs just when *Adonai* begins to give B'nei Yisarel instructions to construct a "temple on wheels" called the *Mishkan*.

Even though *Adonai* is everywhere, our surroundings have a strong influence on how easy or challenging it is to feel God's presence at a given time. It is probably more difficult to feel God's presence in while going through your locker in between classes with a noisy hallway behind you when compared to being in a *minyan* when everyone is quietly reciting the *Amidah*. Imagine, then, the nation of Israel who had spent hundreds of years being exposed to Gods that could be seen and even touched on a daily basis. While they may have been able to recognize that they were being cared for by a deity that preferred not to be carved in stone or wood, the Golden Calf exposed the fact that they still needed something tangible in order to make the connection with and express themselves to *Adonai*.

While B'nei Yisrael may have been familiar with seeing priests conduct prayer-like rituals in the temples of Egypt, they were probably most familiar with the idea of using an offering (animal, plant, even flour) as way to communicate one's intent to a god; and in *Adonai's* system, it could not be just any offering. A sacrifice offered to ask forgiveness for an *Averah*, a transgression, could come in different forms depending on whether the person committed the act on purpose or by accident. An entirely different offering would be given as an expression of thanks, or to make a special request of God. There were the offerings that were part of set rituals conducted by the *Kohanim*, given twice each day with extra offerings for Shabbat and other holidays, and the *Pesah* offering required of every household on the annual celebration of the Jewish people's final night in Egypt.

There were two things that kept an Israelite from just going out behind his tent and giving an offering whenever he wanted to. First, this was an illegal act; in multiple places in the Torah God makes it clear that offerings are only to be given on the altar that God has chosen - the altar that was built for the *Mishkan*, and later given a permanent home in the Temple in Jerusalem. Second, *Adonai* makes it very clear (*Shmot* 25:8) that the purpose of the *Mishkan* is for God to have a place to "dwell among" B'nei Yisrael. While the idea of God "dwelling" in one specific place is in conflict with the idea that God is constantly around us, the people whose only experience with any God was the paganism of the Egyptians would have expected their God to have a physical home among the people. Once *Adonai* announced that the *Mishkan* would be God's dwelling place, it became the only sensible place for an Israelite's "voice" to be heard through the act of giving a offering on its altar.

From the Exodus until the destruction of the First Temple in 586 BCE - about 1000 years - the primary form of communication an individual member of B'nei Yisarel could have with God was the system of offerings and rituals run by the *Kohanim,* first in the *Mishkan* and then, from King Solomon onward, in the Temple itself. While there were multiple prophets conveying God's will to the people throughout this time period the give and take between leaders of B'nei Yisrael and *Adonai* peaked with *Moshe* and never really returned. Keep in mind that this relationship was only for *Moshe* and other leaders; B'nei Yisrael always needed some middleman (*Moshe,* a *Kohen,* or a prophet) to communicate with God.

Before the destruction of the Temple in 586 BCE the ritual life of the average Israelite was much less busy than our ritual life today. The only times someone would engage in worship were either the pilgrimage holidays on the calendar - *Pesah, Shavuot,* and *Sukkot* - or if some action or experience required the giving of an offering. Otherwise the entire nation counted on the *Kohanim* to keep the relationship between B'nei Yisrael and *Adonai* in good working order. A great example of this is *Yom Kippur.* While today every Jew who goes to services on *Yom Kippur* is involved in the act of repentance, during the time of the Temple the job of atoning for the transgressions of B'nei Yisrael fell to the *Kohen Gadol* (High Priest). While the entire nation fasted it was only this single representative of the people who would spend the day engrossed in rituals the outcome of which was forgiveness from God and another year of survival in Eretz Yisrael.

The destruction of the First Temple rocked the ritual life of B'nei Yisrael to its core. For the first time in the peoples' collective memory there was no way to officially reach out and make contact with God; not only did the people feel abandoned by *Adonai*, but they now had no way to reach out to God and ask for forgiveness. It was to fill this vacuum of worship and communication that the leaders of B'nei Yisrael in the Babylonian Galut began to compose what eventually turned into *Tefillah*, the Jewish system of prayer.

As was pointed out in some of the texts earlier in this book, B'nei Yisrael have a historical pattern of being exiled, crying out to God, and then being brought back to Eretz Yisarel. First for the leadership of B'nei Yisrael in Babylon and then for the Rabbis who led the community under Roman rule, there was no question that the pattern could be repeated again. As a result, *Tefillot* were probably viewed by the original authors as a temporary measure, and not a permanent system of worship; one of the most common themes in *Tefillah* is returning to Eretz Yisrael and re-establishing Jewish rule over the land.

The next set of Texts highlight some of the ways in which we use *Tefillah* to reach out to God and ask for Geulah redemption. As you read, keep the following question in mind:

What would you prefer - a return to offerings as our primary mode of communicating with God, or continuing the use of *Tefillah* even after Geulah takes place?

TEXT 23

מפני חטאינו גלינו מארצנו ונתרחקנו מעל אדמתנו

Because of our sins we were exiled from our land and taken far away from our soil;

ואין אנו יכולין לעשות לפניך את קרבנות חובותינו ולהשתחוות לפניך בבית בחירתך בבית הגדול והקדוש שנקרא שמך עליו

And now we have no way to present our sacrifices before you or to bow before you in your chosen house
the Kadosh and great house in which your name was called out

מפני היד שנשתלחה במקדשך

because of the hand that was sent against your sanctuary...

מוסף לשלוש רגלים Selection from *Musaf* for Festivals

TEXT 24

ראה בעניינו וריבה ריבנו וגאלנו מהרה למען שמך כי גואל חזק אתה ברוך אתה ה' גואל ישראל

See our suffering
and fight our disputes
and redeem us quickly for the sake of your name
for you are one who can redeem us with strength.
You are blessed, Adonai who is the redeemer of Israel.

עמידה לימי חול Weekday *Amidah*

What do you think the author of the paragraph that starts with "because of our sins" meant?

Are we supposed to assume that every time the Jewish people suffer it is as a punishment, or is there something more complex going on?

If redemption is guaranteed, and we have not yet been redeemed, what do you think God is waiting for?

Activity: Tefillah for Israel

When we are not giving offerings the primary way in which we express ourselves to God is through the words of Tefillah. Write a Tefillah asking for a return to Israel and Jerusalem. Here are some elements that are common in Tefillah:

- References to what God has done or promised in the past (acknowledging God's power and our status in relation to God)
- References to the current status of the Jewish community
- A request or respectfully worded demand
- Details of how we will know when the request has been fulfilled (example - traditional Tefillot often mention giving sacrifices once again as a measure of redemption)

As you write your Tefillah think about what a return to the Land of Israel really means. Will we re-establish sacrifices in Jerusalem? Will we all worship God in the same way? What kind of government will we form in the era of redemption? Try to work your opinion on all of these questions into the text of your Tefillah.

If he tarries, I will wait...

Activity: What is the Mashiach?

Have you ever heard of the Mashiach?
Together with a partner, write down everything you believe or have heard about the Mashiach below. Then split up, and compare notes with other people in your group.

Some things to think about:
Does Machiach exist?
Is he a normal human being or something more?
What world or Jewish events will cause the Mashiach to arrive?
What world or Jewish events will the Mashiach bring about?

By following the rabbinic system of *Tefillot* the Jewish people were constantly reminded ourselves that we were living in Galut but that one day, with God's help, we would return. Without this strong belief in Geulah it is very likely that we would have been absorbed into the larger nations and become just another footnote in history. This is true when we talk about times in which B'nei Yisrael did not have it so bad in the Galut but it especially applies when times were hard.

When we as a people have been at our lowest point, broken and beaten to the ground, even the comforting words of *Tefillot* have not been enough. It is all very well and good to believe in Geulah in general and participate in the Brit on a regular basis, but how would an individual Jew keep the faith for some general idea of return set sometime in the mists of the future when she was dealing with constant suffering and persecution. It is in trying times that we as a people have needed the specifics of what form Geulah might take.

There seem to be two guarantees made by God in various ways in the *Tanakh*:
1. There is always a way for B'nei Yisrael to be forgiven.
2. With full forgiveness comes the opportunity to return to Eretz Yisrael.

It was after the destruction of the Second Temple in 70 CE that the idea of an individual who would be able to set Geulah in motion took hold. By the time the Talmud was edited together 430 years later there were already an assortment of opinions among the rabbis as to who this person would be and what role he (it was always a male) would play in the process of redemption. Taking most of our cues from statements about Geulah in the book of *Yishayahu* and with contributions from the Talmud and major rabbis such as *Rambam* we have developed many, often conflicting, ideas of just who (and what) the *Mashiach* is and what role, if any, he will play in Geulah.

Before looking at texts and ideas on the *Mashiach* it is important to understand what the word means:

Mashiach - Literally, one who is anointed.

This term originally referred to any leader in B'nei Yisrael who was anointed with oil as part of assuming the leadership role. This list included Kings and the *Kohen Gadol*, the High Priest.

Since monarchy was the only form of Jewish government B'nei Yisrael were accustomed to by the time the Second Temple was destroyed, it was assumed by the rabbis that Geulah would mean a return of Jewish kings to Eretz Yisrael. The original belief in a Mashiach was that there would once again be a king, from the bloodline of David, ruling in Jerusalem.

As time went on an entire mythology began to spring up about the Mashiach giving him special powers. In some stories he is a being in the heavens, just waiting for the moment when God declares B'nei Yisrael to be ready and he can emerge to lead us back to the land. *Eliyahu* the prophet figures into many of these stories as the person who will announce that the Mashiach has arrived and it is finally time for Geulah

So just what is the Mashiach and where does he fit into your beliefs?

TEXT 25

א נַחֲמוּ נַחֲמוּ, עַמִּי--יֹאמַר, אֱלֹהֵיכֶם

1 "Be comforted, be comforted, my nation," says our God.

ב דַּבְּרוּ עַל-לֵב יְרוּשָׁלִַם, וְקִרְאוּ אֵלֶיהָ--כִּי מָלְאָה צְבָאָהּ, כִּי נִרְצָה עֲוֺנָהּ: כִּי לָקְחָה מִיַּד יְהוָה, כִּפְלַיִם בְּכָל-חַטֹּאתֶיהָ.

2 Tell Jerusalem to take heart, and proclaim to her that her time of service has been fulfilled; That her guilt is paid off; That, form God's hand, her sins have been doubly repaid.

ג קוֹל קוֹרֵא--בַּמִּדְבָּר, פַּנּוּ דֶּרֶךְ יְהוָה; יַשְּׁרוּ, בָּעֲרָבָה, מְסִלָּה, לֵאלֹהֵינוּ

3 A voice cries out: "[you] in the desert make way for Adonai, make a desert highway for our God!"

ד כָּל-גֶּיא, יִנָּשֵׂא, וְכָל-הַר וְגִבְעָה, יִשְׁפָּלוּ; וְהָיָה הֶעָקֹב לְמִישׁוֹר, וְהָרְכָסִים לְבִקְעָה

4 Every valley shall be lifted up, and every mountain and hill shall be made low; and the rugged shall be made level, and all the rough places a plain;

ה וְנִגְלָה, כְּבוֹד יְהוָה; וְרָאוּ כָל-בָּשָׂר יַחְדָּו, כִּי פִּי יְהוָה דִּבֵּר

5 And the glory of Adonai shall be revealed, and all flesh shall see it together; for the mouth of Adonai has spoken it.

ישעיהו מ : א-ה   Isaiah Chapter 40, Verses 1-5

We know that redemption will be good for us, the Jewish people, as it will bring us back home. According to this text, how will the redemption benefit God?

In verse two, it states that the sins of Jerusalem have been "doubly repaid." Is it fair of God to punish the Jewish people in a way that goes beyond our original transgressions? Is the destruction of Jerusalem the only punishment, or do you think there is more involved?

How do you feel about the fact that God is telling us to "be comforted" when God is responsible for the punishments in the first place?

Does this text specify what form redemption will take? Why or why not?

א עוּרִי עוּרִי לִבְשִׁי עֻזֵּךְ, צִיּוֹן : לִבְשִׁי בִּגְדֵי תִפְאַרְתֵּךְ, יְרוּשָׁלִַם עִיר הַקֹּדֶשׁ-- כִּי לֹא יוֹסִיף יָבֹא-בָךְ עוֹד, עָרֵל וְטָמֵא

1 Awake, awake, Zion, put on thy strength; put on your beautiful garments, Jerusalem, the holy city; for from now on the uncircumcised and the Tamei there shall no longer enter you.

ב הִתְנַעֲרִי מֵעָפָר קוּמִי שְּׁבִי, יְרוּשָׁלִָם ; הִתְפַּתְּחוּ הִתְפַּתְּחִי מוֹסְרֵי צַוָּארֵךְ, שְׁבִיָּה בַּת-צִיּוֹן.

2 Shake yourself from the dust; arise, and sit down, Jerusalem; loosen the bands around your neck, captive daughter of Zion.

ג כִּי-כֹה אָמַר יְהוָה, חִנָּם נִמְכַּרְתֶּם ; וְלֹא בְכֶסֶף, תִּגָּאֵלוּ.

3 For Adonai says: "You were sold for nothing; and you shall be redeemed without money.

ד כִּי כֹה אָמַר אֲדֹנָי יְהוִה, מִצְרַיִם יָרַד-עַמִּי בָרִאשֹׁנָה לָגוּר שָׁם ; וְאַשּׁוּר, בְּאֶפֶס עֲשָׁקוֹ

4 For this is what Adonai our God says: "In the past my people went down into Egypt to live there; and the Assyrian oppressed them without cause.

ה וְעַתָּה מַה-לִּי-פֹה נְאֻם-יְהוָה, כִּי-לֻקַּח עַמִּי חִנָּם ; מֹשְׁלָו יְהֵילִילוּ נְאֻם-יְהוָה, וְתָמִיד כָּל-הַיּוֹם שְׁמִי מִנֹּאָץ

5 Now therefore, what am I doing here," says Adonai, "seeing that My people is taken away for nothing? They that rule over them howl," says Adonai, "and My name is cursed every day at all times.

ו לָכֵן יֵדַע עַמִּי, שְׁמִי ; לָכֵן בַּיּוֹם הַהוּא, כִּי-אֲנִי-הוּא הַמְדַבֵּר הִנֵּנִי.

6 Therefore My people shall know My name; therefore they shall know in that day that I, God, am the one who spoke - here I am!"

ז מַה-נָּאווּ עַל-הֶהָרִים רַגְלֵי מְבַשֵּׂר, מַשְׁמִיעַ שָׁלוֹם מְבַשֵּׂר טוֹב-- מַשְׁמִיעַ יְשׁוּעָה ; אֹמֵר לְצִיּוֹן, מָלַךְ אֱלֹהָיִךְ

7 How beautiful upon the mountains are the feet of the messenger of good tidings, announcing peace, the sign of good tidings, that announce salvation; that say to Zion: 'your God reigns!'

ח קוֹל צֹפַיִךְ נָשְׂאוּ קוֹל, יַחְדָּו יְרַנֵּנוּ : כִּי עַיִן בְּעַיִן יִרְאוּ, בְּשׁוּב יְהוָה צִיּוֹן

8 Look, your guards! they lift up the voice, together they sing; for they shall see, eye to eye, Adonai returning to Zion.

ט פִּצְחוּ רַנְּנוּ יַחְדָּו, חָרְבוֹת יְרוּשָׁלִָם : כִּי-נִחַם יְהוָה עַמּוֹ, גָּאַל יְרוּשָׁלִָם

9 Break out in joy, sing together, the desolate places of Jerusalem; for the Adonai has comforted God's people, God has redeemed Jerusalem.

י חָשַׂף יְהוָה אֶת-זְרוֹעַ קָדְשׁוֹ, לְעֵינֵי כָּל-הַגּוֹיִם ; וְרָאוּ, כָּל-אַפְסֵי-אָרֶץ, אֵת, יְשׁוּעַת אֱלֹהֵינוּ.

10 Adonai has bared God's holy arm in the eyes of all the nations; and all the ends of the earth shall see the salvation of our God.

ישעיהו נ"ב:א-י   Isaiah Chapter 52, Verses 1-10

Who is being excluded from entering Jerusalem according to verse 1. Why? Do you agree with this sort of exclusion?

What benefit is there to God according to this text when God redeems us? (look at verses 5 and 6)

According to verse 7, how will we know that it is time for redemption? Does this idea seem related to any ideas you know about Mashiach?

אמר רבי חמא בר חנינא : אין בן דוד בא
עד שתכלה מלכות הזלה מישראל

Rabbi Hama, son of Hanina, says: "The son of David will not come until the wicked rulers are kicked out of Israel."

אמר זעירי אמר רבי חנינא : אין בן דוד
בא עד שיכלו גסי הרוח מישראל

Rabbi Ze'iri quotes Rabbi Hanina as having said: "The son of David will not some until the rough winds are gone from Israel."

אמר רבי שמלאי משום רבי אלעזר ברבי
שמעון : אין בן דוד בא עד שיכלו כל
שופטים ושוטרים מישראל

Rabbi Simla'i said in the name of Rabbi Eliezer, quoting from Rabbi Shimon: "The son of David will not come until all the (foreign) judges and officers are gone from Israel."

אמר עולא : אין ירושלים נפדית אלא
בצדקה

Ula said: "Jerusalem will not be rescued by anything except Tzedakah."

אמר רבי יוחנן : אם ראית דור שצרות
רבות באות עליו כנהר - חכה לו

Rabbi Yonatan Said: "If you [are part of] a generation whose troubles come upon them like a river - still, wait for him (Mashiach)."

ואמר רבי יוחנן : אין בן דוד בא אלא בדור
שכולו זכאי, או כולו חייב

Rabbi Yonatan Said: "The son of David will not come except to a generation in which either everyone is innocent, or everyone is guilty..."

סנהדרין דף צ״ח עמוד ב   *Sanhedrin* page 98 side B

Which rabbi's statement do you think makes the most sense?

When Rabbi Hama speaks of "wicked rulers," could he be speaking of Jewish as well as non Jewish leadership?

Why do you think Rabbi Yochanan insists that Mashiach will only come at a time of extremes - either universal guilt or universal innocence?

The following is from a commentary that Rambam wrote about a section of the Mishnah called "Sanhedrin." In this commentary Rambam proposes that there are thirteen foundations of Jewish belief, and spends time exploring each foundation in detail. This, the twelfth foundation, requires a belief in Mashiach:

The Twelfth Foundation is the time of the *Moshiach* (literally, the anointed). This means to believe and be certain that he will come, and not to think that he is late in coming... You should not set a time for him, and you should not make calculations in Scripture to determine the time of his coming. [This foundation further includes] to believe that he (*Moshiach*) will possess advantages, superiority, and honor to a greater degree than all the kings that have ever existed, as was prophesied regarding him by all the prophets, from Moshe, peace be upon him, till Malachi, peace be upon him. One who doubts this or who minimizes his greatness denies the Torah that testifies explicitly to [the coming of Moshiach] in the account of Balaam (BaMidbar [Numbers] 24) and in the portion of *Netzavim* (Devarim [Deuteronomy] 30:3-5). Included in this principle is that there is no king to the Jewish people except from the House of David and the seed of Solomon alone. Anyone who disagrees with [the status of] this family denies God and His prophets.

והיסוד השנים עשר ימות המשיח, והוא להאמין ולאמת שיבא ואין לומר שנתאחר אם יתמהמה חכה לו, ואין לקבוע לו זמן, ולא לפרש את המקראות כדי להוציא מהן זמן בואו, אמרו חכמים תפוח דעתן של מחשבי קיצין. ולהאמין בו מן הגדולה והאהבה ולהתפלל לבואו בהתאם למה שנאמר בו על ידי כל נביא, ממשה ועד מלאכי. ומי שנסתפק בו או זלזל בעניניו הרי זה מכחיש את התורה שהבטיחה בו בפירוש בפרשת בלעם ואתם נצבים. ומכלל היסוד הזה שאין מלך לישראל אלא מדוד ומזרע שלמה דוקא. וכל החולק בענין המשפחה הזו הרי זה כפר בה׳ ובדברי נביאיו. והיסוד השלשה עשר תחיית המתים וכבר ביארנוהו

רמב״ם על סנהדרין פרק י — Rambam's commentary on *Sanhedrin* chapter 10

All sorts of rabbis have tried to calculate exactly when the Mashiach will arrive. Why do you think Rambam frowns on this practice?

Rambam here repeats a concept from the Talmud, that we must constantly wait for the Mashiach. Why do you think the idea of patiently waiting is emphasized so strongly in these texts?

Do you agree with Rambam that is is a requirement of Jewish law to believe in the coming of a Mashiach?

Some final questions:

If there is a Mashiach, do you think he will take the form of a King, or be a part of the modern Israeli democracy?

Do you think we will rebuild the Temple and go back to animal sacrifice, or will we continue to create alternatives to sacrifice? What would you prefer?

The Mashiach is always portrayed as a male. Do you think the Mashiach could be a female, given that in Jewish tradition only males ruled over the Israelite kingdom?

One major assumption made in many of the later texts about Mashiach is that he is someone we are meant to wait for - that when the time is right, we will know, and we will be redeemed. One of the most clear statements of this idea is from an adaptation of *Rambam*'s principles of faith, which takes each of 13 philosophical essays by *Rambam* and distills them into one line. The line dealing with Mashiach may be on you have heard before:

TEXT 29

אני מאמין באמונה שלמה בביאת המשיח ואף על פי שיתמהמה עם כל זה אחכה לו בכל יום שיבא

I believe with full confidence that the Mashiach will come; even if he is delayed, with all that, I will wait for him in every day to some.

The message conveyed in this statement, which many Jews recite daily as part of *Shaharit*, is that our role regarding Geulah and Eretz Yisrael and is a passive one. We are to follow the Brit to the best of our ability, and we will be told when to go back. An adherence to passivity persisted throughout most of the time we spent in Galut after the Second Temple was destroyed. While there were always Jews living in Eretz Yisrael and trying to make their way there, any serious efforts to re-establish Jewish control over the land were few and far between. Most Jews continued to live wherever life had brought them, observing the laws and saying their *Tefillot*, always hopeful that one day the Geulah would arrive. In the meantime, B'nei Yisrael put down roots worldwide, everywhere moving back and forth between wealth and poverty, being welcomed and being expelled.

Part Two—Modern Zionism

Activity: Zionism Is...

Before we learn about some of our early Zionists, let's take a moment to define Zionism. To me Zionism is:

_____

_____

I am a Zionist because

_____

_____

God Helps Those...

By the mid 1800s, the Jews of Europe began to be known to many as a "Nation within a nation." Even those Jews who gave up all of their Judaism and became secularized as much as possible had to face mistrust from the non-Jewish community. Jewish leaders and thinkers constantly dealt with a conflict between being a patriotic Frenchman, for example, while still maintaining a strong Jewish identity. Modern Zionism was born from this conflict.

There were three streams of thought that all developed together in the 1800s, and all converged to eventually helped lead to the creation of Medinat Yisrael These three different streams, each its own brand of Zionism, can be identified as Political, Cultural, and Religious.

Political Zionism

The political Zionists saw a Jewish homeland as a place where the Jewish people could take their place among the nations of Europe. They believed that only by establishing a political entity run by Jews could we ever be completely emancipated. Political Zionists saw a Jewish state as a place that would be just like every other secular, European state, except that it would be set aside for Jews. Theodore Herzl was the key figure in Political Zionism

Theodore Herzl

We are as different as any nation is different from another. We must now create the condition to become a nation like the nations of Europe. This means that the Jews must reclaim their ancient land, to gradually leave the places of dispersion and recongregate in the homeland and, of great importance, to make certain and in advance, that the world recognizes their legal right to do so...

I consider the Jewish question neither a social nor a religious one, even though it sometimes takes these and other forms. It is a national question, and to solve it we must first of all establish it as an international political problem to be discussed and settled by the civilized nations of

---

Theodore (Binyamin Ze'ev) Herzl (1860-1904)
Political Zionism

Viennese journalist and founder of modern political Zionism
Herzl was the first to call for immediate political action to create a safe haven for the Jewish people in their own homeland. He convened the first Zionist Congress in Basel, Switzerland in 1897, chaired the first six Zionist congresses and spent much of his time in his remaining years meeting with world leaders, both Jewish and non-Jewish, trying to enlist financial and political support for his dream of a Jewish state.
Famous phrase: "If you will it, it is no dream"

When have you felt conflicted with the notion of dual identity as a Jewish North American?

Can you think of examples when your religious and national identities have been in conflict? (i.e. basketball tryouts on Yom Kippur)

How did political Zionism aim to fix these issues?

What did Herzl mean when he said that he wanted the Jews to "gradually leave the places of dispersion and recongregate in the homeland?" Did he expect every Jew to move to the Jewish homeland?

In 1947, the "civilized nations of the world in council," the newly formed United Nations, voted that a Jewish state be established where Israel stands today. Do you think, as Herzl seemed to, that a Jewish state has to have the approval of the world political community?

> **Leo Pinsker (1821-1891)**
> *Political Zionism*
> Pinsker believed that the Jewish problem could be resolved if the Jews attained equal rights. As a professional physician, Pinsker preferred a medical term, "Judeophobia," to a recently introduced "anti-Semitism". His analysis of the roots of this ancient hatred led him to call for the establishment of a Jewish National Homeland, either in Palestine or elsewhere. Eventually Pinsker came to agree that hatred of Jews was rooted in the fact that they were foreigners everywhere except their original homeland, the Land of Israel. He became one of the founders and a chairman of the Hovevei Zion movement.

Leo Pinsker

One of the other major thinkers of political Zionism who pre-dated Herzl was Leo Pinsker. Pinsker was a physician, a Zionist pioneer and activist, and the founder and leader of the Hovevei Zion (Lovers of Zion) movement.

The Jews are not a living Nation; they are everywhere aliens; therefore they are despised. The civil and political emancipation of the Jews is not sufficient to raise them in the estimation of the peoples. The proper and the only remedy would be the creation of a Jewish nationality, of a people living on its own soil, the auto-emancipation of the Jews; their emancipation as a nation among nations by the acquisition of a home of their own...The present movement is more favorable than any other for realizing the plan here unfolded...A way must be opened for the national regeneration of the Jews by a congress of Jewish notables.
From Auto-Emancipation, by Leo Pinsker, 1882

What is Pinsker's reasoning for why the Jews need a land?

Many people feel that we are more accepted today than the emancipated Jews of Europe were 100 years ago. What examples can you think of which would confirm or dispute this assumption?

Do you feel this need to "emancipate" yourself as a Jew?

Cultural Zionism

Where Herzl saw the Jewish state as a political need for a place for the Jews to be a nation like every other nation in Europe, men such as Ahad Ha'am saw a Jewish homeland as fulfilling a need to once again create a cultural Judaism. Though not observant Jews, men like Ahad Ha'am and Eliezer Ben Yehudah saw the land of Israel as being essential to the survival of the Jewish people. They envisioned Israel as a land that Jews around the world would turn to for cultural inspiration and guidance, a center for Jewish art and intellect.

Cultural Zionism sees Israel not as a mass living-space for Jews, but as a center for the Jewish battle against assimilation.

<table>
<tr><td>

Ahad Ha'am (1856-1927)
Cultural Zionism
Although secular, Ahad Ha'am (Asher Ginsberg) was deeply committed to the Jewish people. In order for Judaism and the Jewish people to survive and solve the crises of physical and spiritual threat, Ahad Ha'am believed that there must be a Jewish state as the spiritual and cultural center of the Jewish people.

Famous Phrase: "More than the Jewish people have kept the Shabbat, Shabbat has kept the Jewish people"

</td><td>

Ahad Ha'am, *The Jewish State and the Jewish Problem*
For this purpose [of revitalizing Jewish culture] Judaism needs at present very little. It needs not an independent state, but only the creation in its native land of conditions favorable to its development; a good sized group of Jews working without hindrance in every branch of culture, from agriculture to handicrafts to science and literature. this Jewish center... will become in the course of time the center of the [Jewish] nation...
From this center the spirit of Judaism will go forth to the (world)... and will breathe new life into [world Jewry] and preserve their unity...
We may be confident that [the people in this spiritual center] will be able to establish a state which will truly be a Jewish state, and not merely a state of Jews.

</td></tr>
</table>

Does Ahad Ha'am see the need for the immediate establishment of a Jewish state?

What does Ahad Ha'am see as the purpose of gathering Jews in Israel? How does this correspond with Herzl's reasoning?

How do you see Israel as being the cultural center of world Jewry?

Eliezer Ben Yehudah

Ben Yehudah felt that the key to the future of the Jewish people was in the creation of a spiritual/cultural center in Eretz Israel and in the revival of Hebrew as the spoken language. These, and not any other principles, were to be the bedrock of Jewish identity in the future:

It is plain for all to see, sir, that our youth is abandoning our language -- but why? Because in their eyes it is a dead and useless tongue. Let us therefore make the language really live again! Let us teach our young to speak it...

But we will be able to revive the Hebrew tongue only in a country in which the number of Hebrew inhabitants exceeds the number of gentiles. Therefore, let us increase the number of Jews in our desolate land; let the remnant of our people return to the land of their fathers; let us revive the nation and its tongue will be revived too!

Eliezer Ben Yehuda (1858-1922)
Eliezer Ben-Yehuda is credited with the revival of Hebrew as a modern tongue spoken by a renascent Jewish nation. He took an ancient language and transformed it to be spoken in contemporary terms.
Famous Phrase:
'Yisrael be'artzo uvilshono'
ישראל בארצו ובלשונו

The rebirth of the nation of Israel in its own land, speaking its own language.

Why do you think Ben Yehudah saw the Hebrew language as one of the essential parts of Judaism?

Do you think that Hebrew has been "revived" from the lack of use since Ben-Yehuda's time? Is this a result of the existence of Israel?

How does a common tongue contribute to one's nationality?

How do you feel when you hear someone on the street in North America speaking Hebrew?

Do you think it is important for a North American Jew to have some knowledge of Hebrew as the international language of the Jewish people? Why?

How do you think the revival of Hebrew as an everyday language could be seen as disrespectful to the holiness of the language used for Torah and Tefillah?

Religious Zionism

Where Ahad Ha'am and Ben Yehudah were attempting to create a Jewish world without an emphasis on the religious aspects of Judaism, another strong group of Zionists was trying to bring religion back into the Jewish world.

There was a conflict among religious Jews that, to some extent, continues until today. On one side stand those who believe in the "Mashiach," the messianic redemption, but that redemption will come in its own time. This group believed that there was no need to return to the land of Israel, for they believed that when it was time to return, God would tell us.

The other group of religious Jews also believed in the Mashiach, but they also believed that it is the right and privilege of the Jews to live in the land of Israel. Even if the Messiah has not come, they felt Israel is still an essential part of the Jewish people and the Jewish religion.

Abraham Isaac Kook

HaRav Avraham Yitzhak Kook came to Eretz Yisrael in 1904 and began to identify with the Zionist ideal and, in opposition to most other rabbis, joined the political movement. The majority of religious leaders believed that there could be no return to Zion before the coming of the Messiah; and the active Zionists were mostly those who had abandoned their traditional religious roles and replaced them with secular, political activities. Rabbi Kook, on the other hand, believed that the return to Eretz Yisrael marked the beginning of divine redemption (athalta di-ge'ullah).

Excerpts from *Lights*, by Harav Avraham Yitzhak Kook

> *Jewish original creativity, whether in the realm of ideas or in the arena of daily life and action, is impossible except in Eretz Yisrael... A Jew cannot be as devoted and true to his own ideas, sentiments, and imagination in the Diaspora as he can be in Eretz Yisrael...*

Religious Zionists also had to deal with all those Jews flocking to Israel who considered themselves "secularists," people who had completely abandoned the Jewish religion.

> **Abraham Isaac Kook (1865–1935)**
> First Ashkenazi chief rabbi of modern Eretz Yisrael, was a unique blend of the traditional and the modern — a deeply religious man who, unlike many of his contemporaries, also took an active interest in day-to-day life. After World War I, he was elected the first Ashkenazi chief rabbi of Palestine. When Abraham Isaac Kook died in 1935, thousands of Jews lined the streets of Jerusalem to mourn the passing of a great scholar, humanitarian, and religious leader.
>
> **Famous Phrase:**
> Just as the Temple had been destroyed, according to the Talmud, because of *sinat hinnam* (undeserved hatred) among Jews, it will be rebuilt only because of *ahavat hinnam*, i.e., love for Jews even if it is undeserved.

Many of the adherents of the present national revival maintain that they are secularists. If a Jewish secular nationalism were really imaginable, then we would indeed be in danger of falling so low [as a nation] as to be beyond redemption.

But Jewish secular nationalism is a form of self-delusion: the spirit of Israel is so closely linked to the spirit of God that a Jewish nationalist, no matter how secular his intentions may be, must, despite himself, affirm the divine. An individual can sever the tie that binds him to life eternal, but the house of Israel as a whole cannot. All of its cherished national possessions-- its land, language, history, and customs -- are vessels of the spirit of the Lord.

It was Rav Kook's belief that each person had a spark of divine hope within himself that helped Rav Kook become respected even among the secular Zionists. No matter what another Jew's beliefs, he always treated them with respect.

What is your impression of the religious Zionists who have settled in Israel since the creation of the state? Is it good, or bad? Why?

How could a secular Zionist has divine intentions, as Rav Kook thought?

<table>
<tr><td>

Rabbi Yehuda Alkalei (1798-1878)

Rabbi Alkalai was a Sephardi Jew and was one of the first to raise the issue of Jewish political independence and the Land of Israel in 1834 in the pamphlet *Shema Yisrael*, ('Hear O Israel'). He proposed a beginning of Jewish settlement in the Land of Israel as a precursor to the Messianic Redemption and tried to establish organizations that would buy and reclaim land for the Jews in Palestine.

</td></tr>
</table>

Minhat Yehudah, Rabbi Yehudah Alkalai

Rabbi Yehudah Alkalai was a Sephardic rabbi who was one of the earliest voices in Zionism. He advocated for Israel as both a positive step toward redemption, and as a place to revitalize Jewish culture:

I wish to attest to the pain I have always felt at the error of our ancestors, that they allowed our holy Temple to be so forgotten. because of this our people was divided into seventy peoples; our one language was replaced by the seventy languages of the lands of exile.

The organization of an international Jewish body is in itself the first step to the redemption, for out of this organization there will come a fully authorized assembly of elders, and from the elders, the messiah... will appear.

The Redemption will begin with efforts by the Jews themselves; they must organize and unite, choose leaders, and leave the lands of exile.

Activity: My Zionist Identity

Based on what you read about Political, Cultural and Religious Zionism on the previous pages, define each type of Zionism and decide which one appeals most to you.

POLITICAL	MY ZIONIST IDENTITY
CULTURAL	
RELIGIOUS	

Zionism Reaches North America

In the late 19th century, thousands of Jews were migrating to North America. Herzl saw America as a place where Jews would find a temporary home, but anti-Semitism would eventually assert itself, much in the same way that it had in Europe. Herzl's Zionism was growing and by the end of the first year post- publication of "The Jewish State," there were 800 clubs and 100,000 members.

Herzl called for the first Zionist Congress. They met in 1897, in an opera house, in Basel, Switzerland. They were originally to meet in Germany, but religious leadership there thought that Zionists were anti-religious and evil. The Zionists, they thought, rose up against God and Jewish tradition because they didn't have the faith to wait for the coming of the Messiah. They were concerned that the strides they had made in Germany would be lost to accusations of false or dual loyalty. The Jew would once again be seen as having two faces, untrustworthy, not loyal to the State, an enemy from within. The Zionist leadership didn't want the first Zionist Congress to be destroyed before it began, and moved it to Basel.

Herzl's message carried to American shores. The ideas took hold and flowered first in the immigrating teeming masses of Russian, Polish and Lithuanian Jewry, not in New York as expected, but in Chicago, Illinois. The Midwestern American landscape had already been furrowed and fertilized for Zionism, not by Jews, by a Christian fundamentalist.

Chicago Zionism's first champion was William Eugene Blackstone, an evangelical layman and successful real estate entrepreneur who was convinced that the restoration of the Jews to Palestine was a critical forerunner to the return of the Christian Messiah. In 1888, Blackstone traveled with his daughter to Palestine. It confirmed his belief that the Jews were "a people chosen by God to manifest His power and His love to ... a world steeped in deepest idolatry."

In 1891, Blackstone drew up a petition calling for the creation of a national homeland in Palestine for the 2 million oppressed Jews of Russia:

> *"According to God's distribution of nations,"* Blackstone's petition read, *"[Palestine] is their home – an inalienable possession from which they were expelled by force. ... Let us now restore them to the land of which they were so cruelly despoiled by our Roman ancestors."*

More than 400 prominent individuals signed Blackstone's appeal, including the publisher of the Chicago Tribune and Melville W. Fuller, Chief Justice of the United States Supreme Court. The petition was submitted to President Benjamin Harrison. *(Chicago: Incubator of American Zionism, American Jewish Historical Society, 2008)*

The first Jewish American Zionist organization was in Chicago, Illinois. It was organized in the mid 1890's. It was called the Chicago Zion Society.

Zionism in America was bitterly opposed by the American Reform and American Orthodox movements. Most American Jews were relatively recent immigrants who had made clear and conscious decisions to choose America over Israel. They didn't yet know where they stood in America and found it to be a confusing, big place. They looked at America as the *Goldene Medina*—the land of golden dreams). They were less concerned about the anti-Semitism in North America because they had experienced that before in Europe. They now had the opportunity to choose to be Jews— or not to be. Most of the new immigrants decided to remain Jews, longing for community. Over time, however, the "ghetto" mentality that was necessary in Europe started to disappear in America and the Jews started to fit in with the other Americans around them. The new American Jews started to realize that if they were going to find their place in American society as Jews, it would have to be with compromise. Conservative Judaism emerged as a reaction to early Jewish reform movements in an attempt to retain clearer links to halacha (Jewish Law) while at the same time adapting it to modern situations.

Zionism, for most American Jews, was the dream of only a very few before World War I. The American Zionist movement by 1910 could claim less then 10,000 members out of 2,000,000 American Jews.

Imagine yourself trying to fit in as a new immigrant to America. You want to become like everyone else, live the American dream, and acculturate. How could or would Zionism fit into this equation?

Were the other Jewish movements in North America wrong to oppose Zionism?

Zionism and The Conservative Movement

The majority of those associated with the Conservative movement right from the beginning were active Zionists. One notable Zionist leader of the Conservative movement was Solomon Schechter.

Born in Romania, Solomon Schechter (1847-1915) eventually moved to the United States to become the second president of the new Jewish Theological Seminary in New York, which became the home of Conservative Judaism. Schechter worked to make JTS more prominent, bringing in excellent faculty and students, as well as building the school's great library. He laid the foundations of the Conservative movement by outlining its core values and mission and in 1913, he founded the United Synagogue of America (now the United Synagogue of Conservative Judaism) which transformed Conservative Judaism from scholarly approach to a Movement. He was a strong advocate for the Zionist cause long before the state was even established and composed a pamphlet in support of Zionism in 1906, entitled "Zionism: A Statement." In this pamphlet, he publicly and powerfully advocated for the commitment and allegiance to the Zionist cause. His Zionist legacy lives on through on ongoing commitment of the Conservative movement to Judaism and Zionism:

> To me personally, after long hesitation and careful watching, Zionism recommended itself as the great bulwark against assimilation. Zionism declares boldly to the world that Judaism means to preserve its life. It shall be a true and healthy life, with a policy of its own, a religion wholly its own, invigorated by sacred memories and sacred environments, and proving a tower of strength and of unity not only for the remnant gathered within the borders of the Holy Land, but also for those who shall, by choice or necessity, prefer what now constitutes the Galut...

Schechter goes on to describe the "Galut" as a place of tragedy—where synagogues don't hold the same meaning as sacred institutions and the holy language of Hebrew is lost. He is frustrated by the fact that most people are so unfamiliar with Jewish literature and thought and describes it not only as a Galut of the Jews, but as a Galut of Judaism.

I belong to that class of Zionists that lay more stress on the religious-national aspects of Zionism than on any other feature peculiar to it. The rebirth of Israel's national consciousness, and the revival of Israel's religion, or, to use a shorter term, the revival of Judaism, are inseparable. When Israel found itself, it found its God. When Israel lost itself, or began to work at its self-effacement, it was sure to deny its God. The selection of Israel, the indestructibility of God's covenant with Israel, the immortality of Israel as a nation, and the final restoration of Israel to Palestine, where the nation will live a holy life on holy ground, with all the wide-reaching consequences of the conversion of humanity and the establishment of the Kingdom of God on earth --- all these are the common ideals and the common ideas that permeate the whole of Jewish literature extending over nearly four thousand years.

"Only when Judaism has found itself, when the Jewish soul has been redeemed from the Galut, can Judaism hope to resume its mission to the world."

The work in which Zionism had to engage first, and in which it will have to continue for many years to come, was the work of regeneration. It had to re-create the Jewish consciousness before creating the Jewish state. In this respect, Zionism has already achieved great things. Foremost of all, Zionism has succeeded in bringing back into the fold many men and women, both here and in Europe , who otherwise would have been lost to Judaism. It has given them a new interest in the synagogue and everything Jewish, and put before them an ideal worthy of their love and their sacrifice....

How do you think the Zionism of religious leaders such as Schechter differed from political Zionists such as Herzl or Ben Gurion?

A Movement Founded Upon Zionism

In 1913, Solomon Schechter laid the foundation for the creation of the United Synagogue of Conservative Judaism (known then as the United Synagogue of America). Schechter's Zionist connection was demonstrated in the preamble to the USCJ Constitution:

"The advancement of the cause of Judaism in America and the maintenance of Jewish tradition in its historic continuity; to assert and establish loyalty to the Torah in its historic exposition; to further the observance of Sabbath and the Dietary Laws; **to preserve in the Service the reference to Israel's past and the hopes for her restoration;** *to maintain the traditional character of the liturgy, with Hebrew as the language of prayer; to foster Jewish religious schools, in the curricula of which the study of the Hebrew language and literature shall be given a prominent place..."*

Rabbi Jerome M. Epstein, the CEO and Executive Vice President of the United Synagogue of Conservative Judaism commented on the relationship of Conservative Judaism and Zionism as Israel turned 50 for a Mercaz newsletter:

The ideology of Conservative Judaism is shaped by Zionism, which has informed the principles of our organizations and has become an important priority on our Movement's agenda...

...Zionism cannot only be for "other Conservative Jews," it must be for every Conservative Jew. For if Zionism is only for "others," it cannot enrich our lives.

...Eretz Yisrael must play a vital role as a generator providing power. Israel continues

to shape the spectrum of Jewish culture, the richness of Jewish living, the height of Jewish spirituality and the depth of Jewish feeling worldwide. Although Judaism developed for most of history without the reality of Eretz Yisrael, the dream of Israel continued to nurture us in the Diaspora. Today, it is the living Israel that moves us towards completeness.

Yet the issue of Jewish spiritual and cultural identity is not only one for the Diaspora. Over the years, large numbers of Israeli Jews have increased their Israeli while decreasing their Jewish identity. Zionism's task thus is to unite the Diaspora and Israel by strengthening all Jews' commitment and Jewish living, based upon our ancestors' heritage and values; it must translate past values into the way we live today....

The "Ideal" Conservative Zionist Jew

Rabbi Epstein later gave an address that was titled, *The "Ideal" Conservative Jew: Eight Behavioral Expectations."*

> *"Many people mistakenly believe that Conservative Judaism is "pick and choose" Judaism -- that there are no rules or expectations. In truth, however, Conservative Judaism is committed to Jewish tradition and to the observance of mitzvot.*
>
> *The teachings of our movement should affect the way we live our lives -- for if Judaism does not shape our daily decisions and lifestyle, then it is meaningless. An ideal Conservative Jew is a striving Jew, one who is always trying to grow in commitment and knowledge. Each of us should continually climb the ladder of observance. Conservative Judaism asks us to learn and to grow.*

Among the items that the "Ideal" Conservative Jew would do, would be to increase ties and connections to Israel.

> *Since its inception, the Conservative Movement has believed in, and helped to further, the cause of Zionism. As Conservative Jews, we must find ways to increase our ties to Israel in concrete ways.*

Rabbi Epstein encouraged Conservative Jews to join Mercaz (the Conservative Zionist Organization which we will read about on the next page), travel frequently to Israel, send your children on Israel programs, support Israel financially, and consider making aliyah (immigrating to Israel).

What do you think it means to "increase ties and connections" to Israel? What other things could you do to strengthen your connection to Israel?

Israel as a Core Value of Conservative Judaism

In 1995, Rabbi Ismar Schorsch, the sixth Chancellor of the Jewish Theological Seminary, published *Sacred Cluster: The Core Values of Conservative Judaism*, outlining what he calls the seven clusters of Conservative Judaism:

*Conservative Judaism is best understood as a **sacred cluster of core values**. No single propositional statement comes close to identifying its center of gravity. Nor does Conservative Judaism occupy the center of the contemporary religious spectrum because it is an arbitrary and facile composite of what may be found on the left or the right. On the contrary, its location flows from an organic and coherent world view best captured in **terms of core values of relatively equal** worth.*

*There are seven such core values, to my mind, that imprint Conservative Judaism with a **principled receptivity to modernity balanced by a deep reverence for tradition**. Whereas other movements in modern Judaism rest on a single tenet, such as the autonomy of the individual or the inclusiveness of God's revelation at Sinai (Torah mi-Sinai), Conservative Judaism manifests a kaleidoscopic cluster of discrete and unprioritized core values. Conceptually they fall into two sets-three national and three religious-which are grounded and joined to each other by the overarching presence of God, who represents the seventh and ultimate core value. The dual nature of Judaism as polity and piety, a world religion that never transcended its national origins, is unified by God. In sum, a total of seven core values corresponding to the most basic number in Judaism's construction of reality.*

> Rabbi Schorsch does not rank or order the values. Do you think certain values should be priority? Read the values and rank them according to which ones you prioritize.

- *The Centrality of Modern Israel*
- *Hebrew: The Irreplaceable Language of Jewish Expression*
- *Devotion to the Ideal of Klal Yisrael*
- *The Defining Role of Torah in the Reshaping of Judaism*
- *The Study of Torah*
- *The Governance of Jewish Life by Halacha*

Activity: In No Particular Order?

Draw a line between the rank number and the core value. Where would you place 'modern Israel?' Which other value (s) would you add?

The Centrality of modern Israel	
Hebrew: The Irreplaceable Language of Jewish Expression	1
Devotion to the Ideal of *Klal Yisrael*	2
The Defining Role of Torah in the Reshaping of Judaism	3
The Study of Torah	4
The Governance of Jewish Life by *Halacha*	5
Belief in God	6
Other _____	7
	8

Selections excerpted from: Sacred Cluster: The Core Values of Conservative Judaism, February 8, 1995, Reprinted Courtesy of The Jewish Theological Seminary, www.jtsa.edu

Mercaz and Masorti

The Conservative movement, from its inception, embraced Zionism and the centrality of Israel in Jewish life. Originally, it did not have a separate Zionist organization because the ideals of Zionism were central to Conservative Judaism. However, as the Modern State of Israel developed, the very powerful Religious Affairs Ministry did not sanction Conservative/ Masorti Judaism, and disqualified its institutions from recognition, authority, and funding. In order to help these institutions enrich the lives of those Israelis who have been disenfranchised and alienated by the "religion of the state", it became necessary to create a new entity that would represent the interests of Conservative/ Masorti Judaism and allow it to make its unique contribution to the quality of religious life in Israel.

Thus, the creation of Mercaz was added to the Conservative movement's formal support of Israel. Mercaz is the Zionist Organization that serves the interests of the Conservative/ Masorti Movement around the world. It is the Zionist conscience of our Movement and the guarantor for proper recognition and funding for Conservative/Masorti programs and institutions around the world. Among other things, Mercaz is the advocate and the force which guarantees religious stream funding that is so vital to our Movement.

In the United States and Canada, Mercaz must serve as the Zionist conscience and Zionist resource for all arms of our Movement. Since the Conservative movement believes that Israel and Zionism are essential components in Jewish life, we maintain an organization whose mission is the promotion of Zionist education and activities, Israel programs for youth and adults, and aliyah.

Mercaz is the Hebrew word for "center" and was chosen because Zionism is central to Conservative Judaism, and because Conservative/ Masorti Judaism can play a central role in enhancing the quality of religious life in Israel, which is currently not embraced by a large part of Israeli society. Masorti Judaism offers meaningful religious alternatives which until recently were missing from the landscapes of Israeli life.

Masorti is the name of the Conservative movement in Israel. Founded in 1979, it is derived from a Hebrew word that means "tradition," and represents a modern and non-coercive approach to traditional Jewish life. It considers itself pluralistic in its commitment to religious tolerance and is dedicated to Jewish tradition and halachah (law) with an open and positive approach to the modern world, to democratic culture and to Zionism. The Masorti movement boasts more than 50,000 members and affiliates of its Kehillot and programs. Noar Masorti (NOAM) is the youth program of the Masorti movement and USY's sister movement.

Mercaz is the Zionist membership organization of the Conservative Movement, the voice of Conservative Jewry within the World Zionist Organization, the Jewish Agency for Israel, the American Zionist Movement and the Jewish National Fund. It supports religious pluralism in Israel and strengthens the connection between Israel and the Diaspora.

Mercaz sees Zionism as an invaluable tool for strengthening Jewish identity and combating assimilation. It calls for linking Jewish communities throughout the Diaspora with Israel through tourism, Jewish education, Hebrew language study, "people-to-people" partnerships, short- and long-term Israel programs and Aliyah.

The only religious institutions which used to be recognized and funded in Israel were those Orthodox institutions sanctioned by the Chief Rabbinate of Israel. And so, the only alternate source for recognition, funding, and support for our Conservative/Masorti synagogues, schools, youth programs, rabbis, teachers, and mohalim, was and is, the World Zionist Organization. Representation in the World Zionist Organization is based upon the number of members in each organization so Mercaz has continued to increase its membership to assure itself a significant representation in the World Zionist Organization, and significant allocations and funding from that body.

Is it our responsibility as North American Conservative Jews to have a strong commitment to the Conservative movement in Israel and Conservative Zionism today?

How are these organizations an integral part of the mission of Conservative Judaism?

What is the role of North American Zionist organizations today?

What responsibility does a North American Zionist organization have to engage North American Conservative Jews?

Activity: Reaching the Diaspora

Both MERCAZ and MASORTI provide projects and services (like resources for Aliyah, social and religious programs, and advocacy for legalization of non-Orthodox life cycle events in Israel). **What else should these organizations be doing as representative bodies of Conservative Zionism?**

MERCAZ
Imagine you are a board member of MERCAZ. Your job is to figure out new and exciting ways to connect North American Conservative Jews to Israel. What new initiatives or program do you think this organization could offer to bring North American Conservative Jews into the Israel conversation?

MASORTI
Imagine you are an involved member of the MASORTI movement in Israel. What programs or ideas do you have that would connect North American Jews to your life in Israel as a Conservative Jew? Is it important for the two communities to connect or do we live our Jewish lives too differently?

The Jerusalem Program

Membership in Mercaz or any other Zionist organization, including USY, assumes the acceptance of the set of ideals and principles known as the Jerusalem Program.

The Jerusalem Program was adopted in 1951 at the 23rd World Zionist Congress and revised by the 27th Zionist Congress in 1968. It was most recently revised at the meeting of the Zionist General Council in June 2004.

The 1951 version was very focused on the building of the state of Israel, the ingathering of exiles in Eretz Yisrael, and the fostering of the unity of the Jewish people. It referred to the integration of immigrants and stimulation of the agricultural and economic development, acquisition of land as property of the people, and intensive work for chalutziut (pioneering). Since Israel was still so young, harnessing funds and private capital investment were key issues. The authors of the Jerusalem Program believed that the Zionist Movement would be strengthened by imparting the values of Judaism and Hebrew.

In 1968, following the military success of the Six-Day War, the emphasis of the Jerusalem Program shifted slightly to reflect the strengthening of Israel based on justice and peace, and the protection of Jewish rights everywhere. It still included the ingathering of Jewish people through aliyah as well as the emphasis on Jewish, Hebrew, and now Zionist educational as well as Jewish spiritual and cultural values.

Zionism and the 2004 Jerusalem Program

What is the purpose of Zionism?

Zionism is the national liberation movement of the Jewish people. It is the common responsibility of the Jewish people for its continuity and future to ensure a Jewish, Zionist, democratic and secure State of Israel. It was Zionism that brought about the State of Israel's establishment. Zionists agree on the set of ideals and principles known as the Jerusalem Program.

The foundations of Zionism are:
- The unity of the Jewish people, its bond to its historic homeland Eretz Yisrael, and the centrality of the State of Israel and Jerusalem, its capital, in the life of the nation

- Aliyah to Israel from all countries and the effective integration of all immigrants into Israeli Society.

- Strengthening Israel as a Jewish, Zionist and democratic state and shaping it as an exemplary society with a unique moral and spiritual character, marked by mutual respect for the multi-faceted Jewish people, rooted in the vision of the prophets, striving for peace and contributing to the betterment of the world.

- Ensuring the future and the distinctiveness of the Jewish people by furthering Jewish, Hebrew and Zionist education, fostering spiritual and cultural values and teaching Hebrew as the national language;

- Nurturing mutual Jewish responsibility, defending the rights of Jews as individuals and as a nation, representing the national Zionist interests of the Jewish people, and struggling against all manifestations of anti-Semitism.

- Settling the country as an expression of practical Zionism.

Understanding the Jerusalem Program

Underline key words and phrases in the version on the previous page. Circle words you would change and write down replacements.

Do all Jews need to believe in Zionism for Judaism to survive and thrive?

If you were using this to encourage youth Aliyah, how would you sell it? How could you use this text to encourage Aliyah and support of Israel beyond the value of Jewish nationalism?

Why do you think the message changed from the original in 1951, to a revision in 1968 and then the current version of 2004?

Zionism has become so much more than building the country and making Aliyah. How has Zionism changed to include a more realistic picture of the Jewish people?

What does Zionism provide for Jews in the Diaspora?

According to the 2004 Jerusalem Program, why should you be a Zionist?

Activity:
21st Century Zionism and the Jerusalem Program

The Jerusalem Program was last revised in 2004. Knowing what you know, imagine yourself on a committee of scholars and experts with the task of redrafting the Jerusalem Program and the definition of Zionism. What would you edit?

Zionism In Canada

Note a reference from well known Israeli-American sociologist, Steven M. Cohen:

"If you want your kids to be strongly connected to Israel, send them to grow up in Canada"

Canada is known as a *mosaic* of different ethnic groups, cultures and faiths as opposed to the *melting pot* of American cultures. Picture the images of a mosaic and a melting pot. What is the difference between the two in terms of identity and how does this affect attachment to Israel? Canadians are loyal to their places of origin and strongly encouraged to maintain their cultural and ethnic ties. Dual loyalty is normal and encouraged. Canadian Jews, therefore, are loyal to Israel as the homeland of the Jewish people, just as an Indian Canadian remains connected to India.

Activity: Mosaic or Melting Pot?

Do you think it's easier to be a Zionist where each culture or ethnic group maintains its own identity (Mosaic) or where they blend into each other (Melting Pot)?

Is Zionism Racism?
Looking at the UN Resolution

In 1975, the UN General Assembly approved a resolution, supported by Arab, African and Soviet states, asserting that **Zionism is racism**. Logically, this declaration nullified the UN resolutions that had brought about the creation of the State of Israel, and formally, denied the right of self-determination to the Jewish people.

Excerpts from the resolution
THE GENERAL ASSEMBLY, RECALLING its resolution 1904 (XVIII) of 20 November 1963, proclaiming the United Nations Declaration on the Elimination of All Forms of Racial Discrimination...its expression of alarm at "the manifestations of racial discrimination still in evidence in some areas in the world, some of which are imposed by certain Governments by means of legislative, administrative or other measures",

RECALLING ALSO that, in its resolution 3151 G (XXVIII) of 14 December 1953, the General Assembly condemned...the unholy alliance between South African racism and Zionism, ... promulgated the principle that "international co-operation and peace require the achievement of national liberation and independence, the elimination of colonialism and neo-colonialism, foreign occupation, Zionism, apartheid and racial discrimination in all its forms, as well as the recognition of the dignity of peoples and their right to self-determination",

> Do you notice a contradiction here? On the one hand, the resolution is declaring 'Zionism as racism.' On the other hand, they are asserting the "dignity of a peoples and their right to self determination." By proclaiming Zionism- the principle of self determination of the Jewish people- as racism, they are denying the right of the Jewish people the same right they recognize for all others! Why have different rules and standards applied to Jews throughout history?

TAKING NOTE ALSO of resolution 77 (XII) adopted by the Assembly of Heads of State and Government of the Organization of African Unity at its twelfth ordinary session, held at Kampala from 28 July to 1 August 1975, which considered "that the racist regime in occupied Palestine and the racist regime in Zimbabwe and South racist structure and being organically linked in their policy aimed at repression of the dignity and integrity of the human being"

TAKING NOTE ALSO of the Political Declaration and Strategy to Strengthen International Peace and Security and to Intensify Solidarity and Mutual Assistance among Non-Aligned Countries, adopted at the Conference of Ministers for Foreign Affairs of Non-Aligned Countries held at Lima from 25 to 30 August 1975, which most severely condemned Zionism as a threat to world peace and security and called upon all countries to oppose this racist and imperialist ideology,

DETERMINES that Zionism is a form of racism and racial discrimination.

The resolution passed 72 to 35 with 32 abstentions.

Jews around the world reacted in uproar, influencing Jewish leaders and Jewish Israelis to reconsider the U.N. as being a moral governing body. It gave Jews and Israeli leaders the feeling that Israel was completely surrounded by enemies and could never expect any support from the international community, reminiscent of German propaganda prior to World War II.

In 1991, following the collapse of the apartheid regime in South Africa and of the former Soviet Bloc, and against the background of the war against Saddam Hussein, this resolution was repealed. However, the same sentiment surfaced again at the Durban conference in South Africa in the summer of 2001.

Activity: Addressing the Resolution

Imagine reading this resolution in the newspaper in 1975. What feelings and emotions would this stir for you? What would you do about it? Keep in mind that this was a mere 27 years after the Holocaust and Israel's independence. The Jewish people at that time were experiencing both the highs and lows of 20th century Jewish history: the intense pain, suffering and travesty of the Holocaust, the triumph and victory of the establishment of Israel and the Six Day War, and the crushing loss of the 1973 Yom Kippur War.

If you could write a letter to the editor of the paper after reading about the resolution, what would you write?

Dear Editor:

_____

_____

_____

_____

_____

_____

_____

_____

_____

_____

_____

_____

_____

_____

Sincerely Yours,

The Ambassador Responds

Below is the address by Israeli Ambassador to the United Nations Chaim Herzog to the General Assembly of the United Nations:

November 10, 1975
Mr. President,

How would you begin to address this issue? Was Herzog wise to reference Kristalnacht? How would you have begun this letter?

It is symbolic that this debate, which may well prove to be a turning point in the fortunes of the United Nations and a decisive factor in the possible continued existence of this organization, should take place on November 10. Tonight, thirty-seven years ago, has gone down in history as Kristallnacht, the Night of the Crystals. This was the night in 1938 when Hitler's Nazi storm-troopers launched a coordinated attack on the Jewish community in Germany, burned the synagogues in all its cities and made bonfires in the streets of the Holy Books and the Scrolls of the Holy Law and Bible. It was the night when Jewish homes were attacked and heads of families taken away, many of them never to return. It was the night when the windows of all Jewish businesses and stores were smashed, covering the streets in the cities of Germany with a film of broken glass which dissolved into the millions of crystals which gave that night its name. It was the night which led eventually to the crematoria and the gas chambers, Auschwitz, Birkenau, Dachau, Buchenwald, Theresienstadt and others. It was the night which led to the most terrifying holocaust in the history of man.

It is indeed befitting Mr. President, that this debate, conceived in the desire to deflect the Middle East from its moves towards peace and born of a deep pervading feeling of anti-Semitism, should take place on the anniversary of this day. **It is indeed befitting, Mr. President, that the United Nations, which began its life as an anti-Nazi alliance, should thirty years later find itself on its way to becoming the world center of anti-Semitism.** Hitler would have felt at home on a number of occasions during the past year, listening to the proceedings in this forum, and above all to the proceedings during the debate on Zionism.

It is sobering to consider to what level this body has been dragged down if we are obliged today to contemplate an attack on Zionism. **For this attack constitutes not only an anti-Israeli attack of the foulest type, but also an assault in the United Nations on Judaism -- one of the oldest established religions in the world, a religion which has given the world the human values of the Bible, and from which two other great religions, Christianity and Islam, sprang.** Is it not tragic to consider that we here at this meeting in the year 1975 are contemplating what is a scurrilous attack on a great and established religion which has given to the world the Bible with its Ten Commandments, the great prophets of old, Moses, Isaiah, Amos; the great thinkers of history, Maimonides, Spinoza, Marx, Einstein, many of the masters of the arts and as high a percentage of the Nobel Prize-winners in the world, in the sciences, in the arts and in the humanities as has been achieved by any people on earth? . . .

The resolution against Zionism was originally one condemning racism and colonialism, a subject on which we could have achieved consensus, a consensus which is of great impor-

Chaim Herzog (born 17 September 1918, died 17 April 1997) served as the sixth President of Israel (1983–1993), following a distinguished career in both the British Army and the Israel Defense Forces (IDF). In 1975 Herzog was appointed Israel's Ambassador to the United Nations, in which capacity he served until 1978.

How do you think the "Zionism is Racism" claim was used to mask anti-Semitism?

Does Anti-Israel mean anti-Semitic?

Was this claim an attack on Jews or an Israel, or both?

tance to all of us and to our African colleagues in particular. However, instead of permitting this to happen, a group of countries, drunk with the feeling of power inherent in the automatic majority and without regard to the importance of achieving a consensus on this issue, railroaded the UN in a contemptuous maneuver by the use of the automatic majority into bracketing Zionism with the subject under discussion.

What grounds does this claim of "Zionsim" is racism" have? Why would someone believe this?

I do not come to this rostrum to defend the moral and historical values of the Jewish people. They do not need to be defended. They speak for themselves. They have given to mankind much of what is great and eternal. They have done for the spirit of man more than can readily be appreciated by a forum such as this one.

I come here to denounce the two great evils which menace society in general and evils are the motivating force behind the proponents of this resolution and their supporters. These two evils characterize those who would drag this world organization, the ideals of which were first conceived by the prophets of Israel, to the depths to which it has been dragged today.

Do you agree with him that his role is not to defend the Jewish people but do denounce the evil of hatred?

The key to understanding Zionism is in its name. The easternmost of the two hills of ancient Jerusalem during the tenth century B.C.E. was called Zion. In fact, the name Zion, referring to Jerusalem, appears 152 times in the Old Testament. The name is overwhelmingly a poetic and prophetic designation. The religious and emotional qualities of the name arise from the importance of Jerusalem as the Royal City and the City of the Temple. "Mount Zion" is the place where God dwells. Jerusalem, or Zion, is a place where the Lord is King, and where He has installed His king, David.

King David made Jerusalem the capital of Israel almost three thousand years ago, and Jerusalem has remained the capital ever since. During the centuries the term "Zion" grew and expanded to mean the whole of Israel. The Israelites in exile could not forget Zion. The Hebrew Psalmist sat by the waters of Babylon and swore: "If I forget three, O Jerusalem, let my right hand forget her cunning." This oath has been repeated for thousands of years by Jews throughout the world. It is an oath which was made over seven hundred years before the advent of Christianity and over twelve hundred years before the advent of Islam, and Zion came to mean the Jewish homeland, symbolic of Judaism, of Jewish national aspirations.

Do these paragraphs stir feeling or emotion for you? Do you relate to Zionsim for any of these reasons?

While praying to his God every Jew, wherever he is in the world, faces towards Jerusalem. For over two thousand years of exile these prayers have expressed the yearning of the Jewish people to return to their ancient homeland, Israel. In fact, a continuous Jewish presence, in larger or smaller numbers, has been maintained in the country over the centuries.

Zionism is the name of the national movement of the Jewish people and is the modern expression of the ancient Jewish heritage. The Zionist ideal, as set out in the Bible, has been, and is, an integral part of the Jewish religion.

Zionism is to the Jewish people what the liberation movements of Africa and Asia have been to their own people.

Zionism is one of the most dynamic and vibrant national movements in human history. Historically it is based on a unique and unbroken connection, extending some four thousand years, between the People of the Book and the Land of the Bible.

In modern times, in the late nineteenth century, spurred by the twin forces of anti-Semitic persecution and of nationalism, the Jewish people organized the Zionist movement in order to transform their dream into reality. **Zionism as a political movement was the revolt of an oppressed nation against the depredation and wicked discrimination and oppression of the countries in which anti-Semitism flourished. It is no coincidence that the co-sponsors and supporters of this resolution include countries who are guilty of the horrible crimes of anti-Semitism and discrimination to this very day.**

Support for the aim of Zionism was written into the League of Nations Mandate for Palestine and was again endorsed by the United Nations in 1947, when the General Assembly voted by overwhelming majority for the restoration of Jewish independence in our ancient land.

The re-establishment of Jewish independence in Israel, after centuries of struggle to overcome foreign conquest and exile, **is a vindication of the fundamental concepts of the equality of nations and of self-determination. To question the Jewish people's right to national existence and freedom is not only to deny to the Jewish people the right accorded to every other people on this globe, but it is also to deny the central precepts of the United Nations.** As a former Foreign Minister of Israel, Abba Eban, has written:

> *"Zionism is nothing more -- but also nothing less -- **than the Jewish people's sense of origin and destination in the land linked eternally with its name. It is also the instrument whereby the Jewish nation seeks an authentic fulfillment of itself.** And the drama is enacted in twenty states comprising a hundred million people in 4 1/2 million square miles, with vast resources. The issue therefore is not whether the world will come to terms with Arab nationalism. The question is at what point Arab nationalism, with its prodigious glut of advantage, wealth and opportunity, will come to terms with the modest but equal rights of another Middle Eastern nation to pursue its life in security and peace."*

The vicious diatribes on Zionism voiced here by Arab delegates may give this Assembly the wrong impression that while the rest of the world supported the Jewish national liberation movement the Arab world was always hostile to Zionism. This is not the case. Arab leaders, cognizant of the rights of the Jewish people, fully endorsed the virtues of Zionism. Sherif Hussein, the leader of the Arab world during World War I, welcomed the return of the Jews to Palestine. His son, Emir Feisal, who represented the Arab world in the Paris Peace Conference, had this to say about Zionism:

> *"We Arabs, especially the educated among us, look with deepest sympathy on the Zionist movement.... We will wish the Jews a hearty welcome home.... We are working together for a reformed and revised Near East, and our two movements complement one another. The movement is national and not imperialistic. There is room in Syria for us both. Indeed, I think that neither can be a success without the other."*

It is perhaps pertinent at this point to recall that when the question of Palestine was being debated in the United Nations in 1947, the Soviet Union strongly supported the Jewish independence struggle. It is particularly relevant to recall some of Andrei Gromydo's remarks:

> *"As we know, the aspirations of a considerable part of the Jewish people are linked with the problem of Palestine and of its future administration. This fact scarcely requires proof.... During the last war, the Jewish people underwent exceptional sorrow and suf-*

*fering. Without any exaggeration, this sorrow and suffering are indescribable. It is diffi-
cult to express them in dry statistics on the Jewish victims of the fascist aggressors. The
Jews in the territories where the Hitlerites held sway were subjected to almost complete
physical annihilation. The total number of Jews who perished at the hands of the Nazi
executioners is estimated at approximately six million....*

*"The United Nations cannot and must not regard this situation with indifference, since
this would be incompatible with the high principles proclaimed in its Charter, which
provides for the defense of human rights, irrespective of race, religion or sex....*

***"The fact that no Western European State has been able to ensure the defence of the
elementary rights of the Jewish people and to safeguard it against the violence of the
fascist executioners explains the aspirations of the Jews to establish their own State.*** *It
would be unjust not to take this into consideration and to deny the right of the Jewish
people to realize this aspiration."*

Define what is meant by "authentic fulfillment of itself." How is this done in Israel?

How sad it is to see here a group of nations, many of whom have but recently freed themselves of colonial rule, deriding one of the most noble liberation movements of this century,

a movement which not only gave an example of encouragement and
determination to the peoples struggling for independence but also actively aided many of them either during the period of preparation for
their independence or immediately thereafter.

Here you have a movement which is the embodiment of a unique pioneering spirit, of the dignity of labor, and of enduring human values, a
movement which has presented to the world an example of social
equality and open democracy being associated in this resolution with
abhorrent political concepts.

We in Israel have endeavored to create a society which strives to implement the highest
ideals of society -- political, social and cultural -- for all the inhabitants of Israel, irrespective
of religious belief, race or sex.

Show me another pluralistic society in this world in which despite all the difficult problems,
Jew and Arab live together with such a degree of harmony, in which the dignity and rights of
man are observed before the law, in which no death sentence is applied, in which freedom
of speech, of movement, of thought, of expression are guaranteed, in which even movements which are opposed to our national aims are represented in our Parliament.

Do you think its natural for people to accuse others of what they themselves are guilty?

The Arab delegates talk of racism. What has happened to the 800,000 Jews who lived for
over two thousand years in the Arab lands, who formed some of the most ancient communities long before the advent of Islam. Where are they now?

The Jews were once one of the important communities in the countries of the Middle East,
the leaders of thought, of commerce, of medical science. Where are they in Arab society
today? You dare talk of racism when I can point with pride to the Arab ministers who have
served in my government; to the Arab deputy speaker of my Parliament; to Arab officers and
men serving of their own volition in our border and police defense forces, frequently com-
manding Jewish troops; to the hundreds of thousands of Arabs from all over the Middle East
crowding the cities of Israel every year; to the thousands of Arabs from all over the Middle
East coming for medical treatment to Israel; to the peaceful coexistence which has developed; to the fact that Arabic is an official language in Israel on a par with Hebrew; to the fact
that it is as natural for an Arab to serve in an Arab country, indeed being admitted to many
of them. Is that racism? It is not! That, Mr. President, is Zionism.

He makes a fine case for how Zi-
onism is inclusive to Arabs but is this really what Zionism means? How is his point accurate that Arab inclusion defines Zionism?

Zionism is our attempt to build a society, imperfect though it may be, in which the visions of the prophets of Israel will be realized. I know that we have problems. I know that many disagree with our government's policies. Many in Israel too disagree from time to time with the government's policies ... and are free to do so **because Zionism has created the first and only real democratic state in a part of the world that never really knew democracy and freedom of speech.**

This malicious resolution, designed to divert us from its true purpose, **is part of a dangerous anti-Semitic idiom** which is being insinuated into every public debate by those who have sworn to block the current move towards accommodation and ultimately towards peace in the Middle East. **This, together with similar moves, is designed to sabotage the efforts of the Geneva Conference for peace in the Middle East and to deflect those who are moving along the road towards peace from their purpose.** But they will not succeed, for I can but reiterate my government's policy to make every move in the direction towards peace, based on compromise.

Does this resonate with you in a post 9-11 world? Have

We are seeing here today but another manifestation of the bitter anti-Semitic, anti-Jewish hatred which animates Arab society. Who would have believed that in this year, 1975, the malicious falsehoods of the "elders of Zion" would be distributed officially by Arab governments? Who would have believed that we would today contemplate an Arab society which teaches the vilest anti-Jewish hate in the kindergartens?... **We are being attacked by a society which is motivated by the most extreme form of racism known in the world today.** This is the racism which was expressed so succinctly in the words of the leader of the PLO, Yassir Arafat, in his opening address at a symposium in Tripoli, Libya: **"There will be no presence in the region other than the Arab presence...."** In other words, in the Middle East from the Atlantic Ocean to the Persian Gulf only one presence is allowed, and that is Arab presence. No other people, regardless of how deep are its roots in the region, is to be permitted to enjoy its right to self-determination.

Look at the tragic fate of the Kurds of Iraq. Look what happened to the black population in southern Sudan. Look at the dire peril in which an entire community of Christians finds itself in Lebanon. Look at the avowed policy of the PLO, which calls in its Palestine Covenant of 1964 for the destruction of the State of Israel, which denies any form of compromise on the Palestine issue and which, in the words of its representative only the other day in this building, considers Tel Aviv to be occupied territory. Look at all this, and you see before you the root cause of the twin evils of this world at work, the blind **hatred of the Arab proponents of this resolution,** and the **abysmal ignorance and wickedness of those who support them.**

Should we expect to always be disliked? Could envy be the root of anti-Israel activities or viewpoints?

The issue before this Assembly is neither Israel nor Zionism. The issue is the fate of this organization. Conceived in the spirit of the prophets of Israel, born out of an anti-Nazi alliance after the tragedy of World War II, it has degenerated into a forum which was this last week described by [Paul Johnson] one of the leading writers in a foremost organ of social and liberal thought in the West as "rapidly becoming one of the most corrupt and corrupting creations in the whole history of human institutions ... almost without exception those in the majority came from states notable for racist oppression of every conceivable hue." He goes on to explain the phenomenon of this debate:

> *"Israel is a social democracy, the nearest approach to a free socialist state in the world; its people and government have a profound respect for human life, so passionate indeed that, despite every conceivable provocation, they have refused for a quarter of a century to execute a single captured terrorist. They also have an ancient but vigorous culture, and a flourishing technology. The combination of national qualities they have assembled in their brief existence as a state is a perpetual and embittering reproach to most of the new countries whose representatives swagger about the UN building. So Israel is*

envied and hated; and efforts are made to destroy her. *The extermination of the Is-raelis has long been the prime objective of the Terrorist International; they calculate that if they can break Israel, then all the rest of civilization is vulnerable to their as-saults....*

"The melancholy truth, I fear, is that the candles of civilization are burning low. The democracy, or even tribal barbarism, as by a false lexicon of political cliches, accumu-lated over half a century and now assuming a kind of degenerate sacerdotal authority.... We all know what they are...."

Over the centuries it has fallen to the lot of my people to be the testing agent of human decency, the touchstone of civilization, the crucible in which enduring human values are to be tested. A nation's level of hu-manity could invariably be judged by its behavior towards its Jewish population. Persecution and oppression have often enough begun with the Jews, but it has never ended with them. The anti-Jewish pogroms in Czarist Russia were but the tip of the iceberg which revealed the inher-ent rottenness of a regime that was soon to disappear in the storm of revolution. The anti-Semitic excesses of the Nazis merely foreshadowed the catastrophe which was to befall mankind in Europe....

On the issue before us, the world has divided itself into good and bad, decent and evil, hu-man and debased. We, the Jewish people, will recall in history our gratitude to those nations who stood up and were counted and who refused to support this wicked proposition. I know that this episode will have strengthened the forces of freedom and decency in this world and will have fortified the free world in their resolve to strengthen it has weakened the United Nations.

As I stand on this rostrum, the long and proud history of my people unravels itself before my inward eye. I see the oppressors of our people over the ages as they pass one another in evil procession into oblivion. I stand here before you as the representative of a strong and flourishing people which has survived them all and which will survive this shameful exhibi-tion and the proponents of this resolution.

The great moments of Jewish history come to mind as I face you, once again outnumbered and the would-be victim of hate, ignorance and evil. I look back on those great moments. I recall the greatness of a nation which I have the honor to represent in this forum. I am mindful at this moment of the Jewish people throughout the world wherever they may be, be it in freedom or in slavery, whose prayers and thoughts are with me at this moment.

I stand here not as a supplicant. Vote as your moral conscience dictates to you. For the is-sue is neither Israel nor Zionism. The issue is the continued existence of this organization, which has been dragged to its lowest point of discredit by a coalition of despots and racists. The vote of each delegation will record in history its country's stand on anti-Semitic racism and anti-Judaism. You yourselves bear the responsibility for your stand before history, for as such will you be viewed in history. We, the Jewish people, will not forget.

For us, the Jewish people, this is but a passing episode in a rich and event-filled history. We put our trust in our Providence, in our faith and beliefs, in our time-hallowed tradition, in our striving for social advance and human values, and in our people wherever they may be. For us, the Jewish people, this resolution based on hatred, falsehood and arrogance, is devoid of any moral or legal value.

Source: Israeli Ministry of Foreign Affairs

Herzog's Response: Think about it!

What do you think was the basis for the "Zionism is Racism" claim?

Which sections agitated you or made you uncomfortable?

How do you feel Herzog's argument still relevant today? Apply it to the situation in the world as we know it.

Does this letter leave you feeling optimistic or realistic?

Herzog is not only defending Zionism and Israel but the Jewish people as a whole. Do you think it is the function of Zionism and its leadership to come to the aid of the Jewish people? Should they react when Israel is attacked, or if there is an attack on all Jews? Do you feel insecure as a Jew when Israel is in danger?

How does the Talmudic phrase "Kol Yisrael arevim zeh ba zeh" (Shevuot 39a) (All Israel is responsible for one another) apply to this document? How does this piece put this phrase into perspective for you? How?

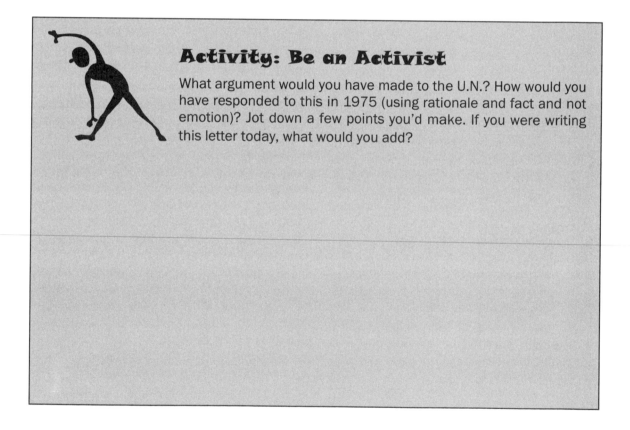

Activity: Be an Activist

What argument would you have made to the U.N.? How would you have responded to this in 1975 (using rationale and fact and not emotion)? Jot down a few points you'd make. If you were writing this letter today, what would you add?

Israel: A Look from the Diaspora

Activity: Where do you fit in?

WHERE DO YOU FIT IN?
What role do YOU think Jews in North America should play regarding Israel?
Should Jews in North America stick their noses into Israeli policies?

"Israelis don't like it when American Jews express their opinions about Israel. American Jews don't live in Israel, don't serve in the army, don't like with the consequences of political decisions. Therefore, the argument goes, they have no right to make their voices heard in the Israeli decision making process"

STRONGLY AGREE				STRONGLY DISAGREE
1	2	3	4	5

"We live in a time when American Jews are becoming increasingly alienated from Israel. Research by American-Israeli sociologist Steven M. Cohen and others has shown that American Jews are less attached to Israel than they were a generation ago, and that young American Jews are the least attached of all"

STRONGLY AGREE				STRONGLY DISAGREE
1	2	3	4	5

"You American Jews are Israel's informal Ambassadors; your job is to support and defend it against detractors..."

STRONGLY AGREE				STRONGLY DISAGREE
1	2	3	4	5

"This passion and deep commitment...were characterized by vociferous debate...Passionate debate goes hand in hand with deep commitment. If American Jews don't feel strongly connected to Israel in the 21st century, then we, as a global Jewish people are in serious trouble, therefore, we need passionate American Jewish debate about Israel"

STRONGLY AGREE				STRONGLY DISAGREE
1	2	3	4	5

"Without change, American Jewry will continue to grow increasingly distant from Israel. The only way to stop this is to encourage American Jews to feel that they are stakeholders in the big issues."

STRONGLY AGREE				STRONGLY DISAGREE
1	2	3	4	5

"American Jews should be encouraged to stick their noses into Israeli policies...because if they stick their noses in, there's a lot more chance that their hearts will follow.

STRONGLY AGREE				STRONGLY DISAGREE
1	2	3	4	5

(Excerpted from "Americans Should Stick Their Noses In" by Alex Sinclair, *Jerusalem Report*, 2007, Used with author's permission)

Is It A Mitzvah To Make Aliyah?

Since the days of the Mishnah 1800 years ago, whenever the Jews have had a serious ethical or legal problem, they send a written question to the rabbi of their choice who wrote a detailed reply based upon the Tanakh, the Babylonian Talmud, commentaries to the Talmud and codes of Jewish law. These Responsa are known as "Sheilot u'Teshuvot (questions and answers) and comprise the body of written decisions and rulings given by the rabbis who have studied the texts and have made decisions about Jewish Law.

A question arose asking "Is it a mitzvah to make aliyah". The first question that had to be asked "What constitutes a mitzvah"? Next, texts regarding aliyah to Israel found in the Tanakh (Hebrew Bible), Talmud and modern rabbinical literature were all taken into account. Finally, a recommendation is made via the "Responsum" (or response) as an answer to the question. Take a look at the full text of the Responsum below on the question "Is it a Mitzvah to Make Aliyah."

QUESTION: Is it a mitzvah to make aliyah? [1]

By Rabbi David Golinkin

* Editor's Note: Text bolded for educational purposes

YD 157:1

RESPONSUM

Rabbi David Golinkin was born and raised in Arlington, Virginia and made aliyah in 1972. He received an M.A. in Rabbinics and a Ph.D. in Talmud from the Jewish Theological Seminary of America where he was also ordained as Rabbi. Prof. Golinkin is President and Professor of Jewish Law at the Schechter Institute of Jewish Studies in Jerusalem. He is long-time Chair of the Va'ad Halakhah (Law Committee) of the Rabbinical Assembly which writes responsa and gives halachic guidance to the Masorti (Conservative) Movement in Israel.

The word *mitzvah* can mean good deed, but, technically, it refers to one of the 613 *mitzvot* or commandments in the Torah. This number was originally stated by Rabbi Simlai in the third century (*Makkot* 23b); [2] since then dozens of rabbis have enumerated the 613 commandments. [3]

As I have explained elsewhere, [4] *Eretz Yisrael* holds a unique place in Jewish tradition and history. As a result, we would expect our tradition to unanimously require *aliyah*. Yet, in fact, rabbinic literature contains at least five different approaches towards *aliyah*:

1. The early midrash of *Sifrei Devarim* (paragraph 80) relates that Rabbi Elazar ben Shamua and Rabbi Yohanan ha-Sandlar (ca. 150 c.e.) were on their way to study Torah outside of *Eretz Yisrael*. When they reached Sidon in Lebanon, they remembered *Eretz Yisrael*. They began to cry and they rent their garments and they recited the verse (Deuteronomy 11:31-32): "When you have occupied it and are settled in it, take care to observe all of the laws. . . " Said they: `Dwelling in *Eretz Yisrael* is equal to all of the other commandments in the Torah'. Whereupon they turned around and went back to *Eretz Yisrael*.

Rabbi Golinkin, David. Responsa in a Moment. Jerusalem: The Institute of Applied Halakhah at the Schechter Institute of Jewish Studies, 2000, pp. 79-83.

NOTES

1. I.e. to immigrate to Israel. There is a vast literature on this subject. In English, see J. K. Mikliszanski, *Judaism* 12/2 (Spring 1963), pp. 131-141; J. David Bleich, *Contemporary Halakhic Problems*, vol. 1, New York and Hoboken, 1977, pp. 3-13: Ephraim Kanarfogel, *Jewish Quarterly Review* 76/3 (January 1986), pp. 191-215; Hershel Schachter in Shubert Spero and Yitzchak Pessin, eds. *Religious Zionism*, Jerusalem, 1989, pp. 190-212.
2. See Nahman Danzig, Sinai 83 (5738), pp. 153-158 for the history of this number.
3. See *Encyclopaedia Judaica*, vol. 5, cols. 760-783.
4. See my responsum in *Moment* 18/6 (December 1993), pp. 34 = above, pp. 31- 32. For the centrality of *Eretz Yisrael* in Jewish tradition, see above, p. 35, note 2.

2. Nahmanides (1194-1270) followed their approach by ruling that it is a positive commandment to inherit the land and dwell therein. [5] Furthermore, he practiced what he preached, arriving in Jerusalem from Spain in 1267 and settling in Acre. [6] His opinion was accepted by a number of prominent medieval rabbis and is very popular among Israeli rabbis today. [7]

On the other hand, the above-mentioned Rabbi Simlai did not view *aliyah* as a *mitzvah* in and of itself but rather as a *makhshir mitzvah* or preparatory act which enables one to perform the *mitzvot* which can only be performed in Israel such as tithing and the Sabbatical and Jubilee years. [8]

Rabbi Simlai expounded: Why did Moses our teacher yearn to enter the land of Israel? Did he want to eat of its fruits or satisfy himself from its bounty? But thus said Moses: "Many mitzvot were commanded to Israel which can only be fulfilled in *Eretz Yisrael*. I wish to enter the land so that they may all be fulfilled by me" (*Sotah* 14a). Rabbi Simlai's approach was also followed by a number of medieval rabbis. [9]

3. Other talmudic sages did not rule explicitly on whether *aliyah* is a *mitzvah*, but tried to encourage *aliyah* and discourage emigration via specific legislation: [10] "Both husbands and wives may force their spouses to make *aliyah* (*Mishna Ketubot* 13:11). If a Jew wants to buy land in Israel, he may tell the non-Jewish owner to draw up the contract even on Shabbat (*Gittin* 8b and *Bava Kamma* 80b). "It is forbidden to leave *Eretz Yisrael* unless two se'ah (26.4 liters) of wheat sell for one *selah*. Rabbi Shimon said. . . if one can find any wheat at all, even if one se'ah costs a *selah*, he should not emigrate" (*Bava Batra* 91a).

Maimonides followed this approach. He codified the specific laws mentioned above, [11] yet he did not list *aliyah* as one of the 613 *mitzvot*. Indeed, Maimonides himself seems to have visited Israel in the year 1165, but did not remain. [12]

4. A number of medieval rabbis took a pragmatic approach. Rabbi Meir of Rothenburg (Germany ca. 1215-1293), for example, did not think that *aliyah* was one of the *mitzvot*, but he did think that whoever moves to Israel "for the sake of heaven and conducts himself in holiness and purity, there is no end to his reward, provided that he can support himself there". [13]

Rabbi Israel Isserlein (Austria, 1390-1460) ruled that it is certainly praiseworthy to live in Israel. However, since there is danger involved and since it is hard to earn a living there, "every person should judge his physical and monetary capabilities if he will be able to fear Heaven and observe *mitzvot* [in Israel]" (*Pesakim U'ketavim*, no. 88).

Do you agree with this statement? If you were to rank Aliyah as one of the top three mitzvot, which other two would you consider?

Can you only live a Jewish life in Israel? Can you live a complete Jewish life in North America? How does being in Israel make you feel more Jewish?

How do you relate to Maimonides' relationship towards Israel? Apply this idea to North American Jewry.

What do you feel are the "rewards" of making Aliyah? What would outweigh the struggle?

5. Nahmanides to Numbers 33:53 and in his addenda to *Sefer Hamitzvot* by Maimonides, no. 4.
6. Regarding Nahmanides' *aliyah*, see Rabbi Charles Chavel, *Ramban: His Life and Teachings*, New York, 1960, pp. 56-66.
7. *Responsa Ribash*, no. 101: *Responsa Tashbatz*, part 3, no. 288; Rabbi Ovadiah Yosef, *Torah Shebe'al Peh* 11 (5729), pp. 35-42; Rabbi Hayyim David Halevi, *Aseh Lekha Rav*, part I, Tel Aviv, 5736, nos. 17-18. This was also the approach of Rabbi Abraham Isaac Kook which has been adopted by most religious Zionists in Israel.
8. For a good summary of the *mitzvot* dependent on the land, see Dayan I. Grunfeld, *The Jewish Dietary Laws*, vol. 2, London, Jerusalem and New York, 1972.
9. Rashbam to *Bava Batra* 91a, s.v. ein yotzin and Rabbi Baruch of Worms, *Sefer Haterumah*, Warsaw, 1897, p. 122a.
10. This legislation was probably a reaction to the dire economic situation after the Bar Kokhba revolt. See Gedaliah Alon, *The Jews in their Land in the Talmudic Age*, Jerusalem, 1984, pp. 659-661.
11. *Ishut* 13:20; *Avadim* 8:9-10; *Shabbat* 6:11; *Melakhim* 5:9-12; *Responsa of Maimonides*, ed. Blau, no. 365.
12. See *Encyclopaedia Judaica*, vol. 11, cols. 755-756. Regarding Maimonides' attitude towards *Eretz Yisrael*, see I. Twersky in Joel Kraemer, ed., *Perspectives on Maimonides*, Oxford, 1991, pp. 257-292.
13. *Responsa of the Maharam of Rothenberg*, ed. Berlin. Nos. 14-15, but cf. ibid. no. 79 where he states that making *aliyah* is indeed a *mitzvah*.

*Does this have
any merit? In
terms of the
economic strug-
gle, do you
think this is a
legitimate rea-
son to not make
Aliyah?*

*How does it
make you feel to
see Jews so
strongly pro-
testing Israel's
existence?*

5. Lastly, there is the lone talmudic voice of the Babylonian sage Rabbi Judah who de-clared that whoever makes *aliyah* from Babylon to Israel actually *transgresses* a posi-tive commandment (sic!). [14]

This negative approach to *aliyah* was followed by quite a few medieval rabbis. [15] **Rabbi Judah the Pious** (Ashkenaz, thirteenth century) ruled, for example, that it is preferable *not* to make *aliyah*, because he who does so will not be able to find a wife in Israel nor have time to study Torah due to the difficult economic conditions. [16]

In modern times, Rabbi Judah's approach has been adopted by the **Satmar Hassidim** who rabidly **oppose mass** *aliyah*, **Zionism and the State of Israel due to their conviction that only God may redeem the Jewish people from Exile.** [17]

Given these five approaches, it is difficult to state *the* halakhic approach to *aliyah*, since all five can be justified by talmudic and halakhic sources. Therefore, I would like to explain *my* halakhic approach to *aliyah*.

I made aliyah in 1972 because I believe that *aliyah* is both a *mitzvah* and a *makhshir mitz-vah*. First of all, Nahmanides was right to list *aliyah* as a *mitzvah*. He remained in the minor-ity only because all attempts to list the 613 *mitzvot* took place at a time when it was virtu-ally impossible for most Jews to make *aliyah*. It seems that most rabbis saw no point in re-quiring something so dangerous and expensive that it was virtually unobtainable. By requir-ing *aliyah*, the rabbis would have turned almost the entire Jewish people into sinners. [18] But the thrust of Numbers 33:53 as well as of the entire Bible and Talmud is *that all Jews are supposed to live in Eretz Yisrael*. That is what God repeatedly promised our ancestors, that is why God redeemed us from Egypt, and that is where a large percentage of the *mitzvot* need to be observed.

Furthermore, *aliyah* is a *mitzvah* in the sense of a **preparatory act because it enables one to perform not only the** *mitzvot* **connected to the land** (no. 2 above) but *all* of the *mitzvot*. In Israel, one can observe Shabbat and all of the Jewish holidays with ease because the en-tire country is on "Jewish time". Israel is conducive to **Torah study** both in terms of vast op-portunities and in terms of **enabling the Bible and the Talmud to come to life.** Living in Is-rael allows one to **master Hebrew** and thereby connect to our heritage which is written in **Hebrew. Israel ensures "Jewish continuity"** because, religious or secular, your children will **most likely marry other Jews.** Finally, Israel is the actualization of the prayers we have re-cited for 2,000 years: "May our eyes behold **Your return to Zion** with mercy"; "Blessed are you **God who gathers the dispersed of Your people Israel".**

In conclusion, one should make *aliyah* because living in Israel is a *mitzvah* in and of **itself as well as a preparatory** act which enables one to **observe all of the** *mitzvot* and to **live a full Jewish life** by living in a Jewish state.

14. *Ketubot* 110b-111a. Space does not allow me to explain the involved Talmudic passage regarding "the three oaths" which follows.

15. See the exhaustive treatment by Aviezer Ravitzky, *Messianism, Zionism and Jewish Religious Radicalism*, Chicago, 1996, pp. 211-234.

16. See Kanarfogel (above, note 1), pp. 205-206. 17. For the Satmar approach, see Ravitzky, chapter 2 and *Encyclopaedia Judaica*, vol. 15, cols. 909-910.

18. Cf. *Bava Kamma* 79b and parallels: "one does not impose a decree on the public unless the majority can abide by it".

Activity: Dare to Compare

Rabbi Golinkin offers a number of perspectives from our great sages to support his own tshuvah on whether it is a mitzvah to make Aliyah. Read the comments of our sages and consider some of the following questions:

1. "Dwelling in *Eretz Yisrael* is equal to all of the other commandments in the Torah"- Rabbi Elazar ben Shamua and Rabbi Yohanan ha-Sandlar

   Do you agree with this statement? If you were to rank Aliyah as one of the top three mitzvot, which other two would you consider? Is Aliyah a consideration for you?

2. "Rabbi Simlai did not view *aliyah* as a *mitzvah* in and of itself but rather as a *makhshir mitzvah* or preparatory act which enables one to perform the *mitzvot* which can only be performed in Israel"-Rabbi Simlai continues, explaining Moshe's reason for wanting to enter Eretz Yisrael:
   "Many mitzvot were commanded to Israel which can only be fulfilled in *Eretz Yisrael*. I wish to enter the land so that they may all be fulfilled by me" (*Sotah* 14a).

   What exactly is this saying? That you can only live a complete Jewish life in Israel? Or that Israel enables you to live Jewishly unlike any other place in the world? Can you live a complete Jewish life in America? Why or why not?

3. "Maimonides followed this approach. He codified the specific laws mentioned above, yet he did not list *aliyah* as one of the 613 *mitzvot*. Indeed, Maimonides himself seems to have visited Israel in the year 1165, but did not remain."

   How do you relate to Maimonides relationship toward Israel? Apply this idea to North American Jews and their relationship to Israel. Can you relate to the "I visit Israel as my homeland but live in the United States or Canada as my home"

4. "...there is no end to his reward, provided that he can support himself there."- Rabbi Meir of Rothenburg

   "Rabbi Israel Isserlein (Austria, 1390-1460) ruled that it is certainly praiseworthy to live in Israel. However, since there is danger involved and since it is hard to earn a living there, 'every person should judge his physical and monetary capabilities if he will be able to fear Heaven and observe *mitzvot* [in Israel]' " (*Pesakim U'ketavim*, no. 88).

   North American Jews are comfortable in North America. Moving to Israel would be a great struggle (and sacrifice) emotionally, financially and physically but is so rewarding on so many levels. What do you feel are the "rewards" of making Aliyah? What would outweigh the struggle of this lifestyle change?

6. "...Rabbi Judah who declared that whoever makes *aliyah* from Babylon to Israel actually *transgresses* a positive commandment (sic!)."
   Imagine you are Rabbi Judah. Explain your comment. How would making *Aliyah* detract from your own Jewish way of life? Do you think you'd make less of an effort to behave Jewishly living in Israel? Do Israelis?

7. "Rabbi Judah the Pious (Ashkenaz, thirteenth century) ruled, for example, that it is preferable *not* to make *aliyah*, because he who does so will not be able to find a wife in Israel nor have time to study Torah due to the difficult economic conditions."

Does this have any merit? Today, many young Jews go to Israel to find just that- a future spouse or significant other and Torah study. In terms of the economic struggle, do you think this is a legitimate reason to not make Aliyah? Think about your (great) grandparents who were immigrants. They too struggled to earn a living upon entering America.

8. "In modern times, Rabbi Judah's approach has been adopted by the **Satmar Hassidim** who rabidly **oppose mass *aliyah*, Zionism and the State of Israel due to their conviction that only God may redeem the Jewish people from Exile.**"

Have you ever witnessed the Satmars at an Israel rally? How does it make you feel to see Jews so strongly protesting Israel's existence? Does it make you stand even firmer in your support for Israel? Is not being supportive of Aliyah therefore supporting the Satmar Hassidim in some way? Why or why not?

9. "But the thrust of **Numbers 33:53 as well as of the entire Bible and Talmud is *that all Jews are supposed to live in Eretz Yisrael*. That is what God repeatedly promised our ancestors, that is why God redeemed us from Egypt, and that is where a large percentage of the *mitzvot* need to be observed.**"

What is Rabbi Golinkin saying here? Is God's eternal covenant with the Jewish people reason enough for a Jew to make Aliyah? How do you relate to the idea of Aliyah as fulfilling God's eternal covenant? Do you connect with Israel as the land of your ancestors? Is there something you believe in so strongly that you would make a decision as great as something like Aliyah?

Activity: Questions and Questions

If you had an opportunity to speak with Rabbi Golinkin, how would you respond to his argument? Which part (s) do you agree with? What questions do you have for this committed and knowledgeable North American Jew who decided to live in Israel so that he can live a full and committed Jewish life, experience Jewish space and time and be able to and perform all mitzvot without barriers?

Can one live a full Jewish life outside of Israel? How do you? What obstacles do you face that you wouldn't necessarily encounter in Israel? What do you feel is missing from your life as a Jewish North American? What do you feel you have in North America that you wouldn't in Israel?

Based on Rabbi Golinkin's opinion and the other responses from our sages, what do you think. Is it a mitzvah to make Aliyah?

Activity: Why Make Aliyah

The Push-Pull Factor

What is pushing you away from North America? Living as a minority in North America, what difficulties do you face?

What is pulling you towards Israel? What types of things do you think would be easier if you lived in Israel?

What are the challenges of living in Israel? What sacrifices would you have to make to move to Israel? Do you think they are worth it? Do the benefits of living in Israel outweigh the costs?

CHALLENGES	SACRIFICES
BENEFITS	COSTS

Activity: Challenges of Aliyah
Part I: What Challenges would you face in making Aliyah?

With these differing perspectives in mind, think of elements of your Jewish self you feel are missing as a Jew in North America (actions or elements of identity such as being a minority) that would be different living in "Jewish space and time" in Israel. What challenges would you face in Israel that you don't face in North America and vice versa? Try listing them below.

Part II: What can you do to make Israel important without Aliyah?

Aliyah may eventually be an option to you however, if this is not something you consider viable, what small changes can you make to have Israel be more of a dominant part of your Jewish self?

Does Israel need Us?

Do you define yourself as a North American Jew? A Jewish American? A Jewish Canadian?

How do you reconcile your dual identity? Do you think Israelis struggle with dual identity or is being Israeli being Jewish?

Answer the following: I would define myself as: _____

As North Americans, is the Jewish state or homeland just in our imaginations- that we "dream of Zion" by living elsewhere? What exactly do we mean when we say 'next year in Jerusalem?' at the Passover Seder?

A.B Yehoshua Lights a Fire

On the evening of May 1, 2006, A.B. Yehoshua, a prominent Israeli novelist addressed a primarily American audience of top Jewish scholars, leaders and academics at the American Jewish Committee Centennial Symposium. "AJC's Centennial Annual Meeting" in Washington opened with a four-part symposium in which prominent Jewish intellectuals addressed the challenges of the Jewish future as well as the meaning of Jewish spirituality, community, and continuity. The first panel was held at the Library of Congress on the evening of May 1, 2006, and included a discussion with top Jewish academics, and A.B. Yehoshua addressing the question, 'What Will Become of the Jewish People?'" Yehoshua's candor shocked the audience:

A.B. Yehoshua is 5th generation native born Israeli (Sabra), a well known Israeli novelist, essayist, and playwright. He is nicknamed "Boolie" in Israel and has won both the Bialik Prize and the Israeli Prize for literature. His novels include: *The Lover, a Late Divorce, The Liberated Bride and A Woman in Jerusalem*.

Excerpts from: A.B. Yehoshua Controversy, An Israel-Diaspora Dialogue on Jewishness, Israeliness, and Identity. *Dorothy and Julius Koppelman Institute on American Jewish-Israeli Relations, American Jewish Committee.* **The Great Debate**: A.B. Yehoshua sparks an international dialogue on the Israel-Diaspora relationship, AJC Centennial Symposium, [excerpts of Foreword by Leon Wieseltier of The New Republic, Ambassador Alfred H. Moses, chair of the ACJ Centennial Committee and Dr. Steven Bayme, Director, Koppelman Institute, AJC] Used with Permission, AJC. A video of the entire dialogue is available at the AJC website at ajcarchive.org - type in Centennial Symposium and look for the videos for May 1, 2006.

The unfeasibility of dual loyalty:

I am what I am. I have a country. I have a language. I have a people. I have a framework. I have a reality...I have a clear identity. I don't see the "other." Who is the "other" that I have to be like him? It's your problem. It's not my problem... have to say to you, I very welcome your [Cynthia Ozick's] dual loyalty, but I ... don't get it.... I would like that you would have one loyalty, in Israel, and participate. The fact that Israel is in your mind, that doesn't help me.

Does it help Israelis to know we are thinking of them and engage is Israel related dialogue consistently?

Why is it that North American Jews seem to visibly support Israel more during times of stability and turn away during times of struggle?

Dina D'malchuta Dina——The law of the land is the law- this concept instructs the Jew that when the law of the land conflicts with Halacha, one must act according to the law of the land and not according to Halacha. **Can you think of any examples?**

Do you ever experience a conflict between American and Jewish values? When do you feel torn between the two? Are there situations when North American Jews make American decisions within a Jewish framework?

Yehoshua continues:

Eventual disappearance of the Diaspora:
"If ... in 100 years Israel will exist and ... I will come to the Diaspora [and] there will not be [any] Jews ... I will not cry ... I don't say I want it.... But if ... Israel will disintegrate ... for me personally ... there is no alternative to be a post-Zionist Jew.... ["I ... will not have [and] cannot keep my identity outside Israel....[Being] Israeli is my skin, it's not my jacket. You are changing jackets—from Argentina you take your jacket to Brazil, from Brazil ... to America, from there, there, and then you're moving. You are changing countries like the Jews have done all the time, changing countries like changing jackets."

What does this mean: "(Being) Israeli is my skin, it's not my jacket"?

How do you think that Jews may eventually disappear into the fabric of the countries in which they live?

Do you sometimes take your Jewish jacket on and off and decide at different points to make your Jewishness more known than at others? Can you do this in Israel?

Do you think Yehoshua stepped over the line here? Was his opinion accurate, or was he being offensive?

Inauthentic American [Diaspora] Judaism:
He went further, accusing Diaspora Jews of "playing with Jewishness" because their decisions as Jews were made in American terms. He referred to Diaspora Judaism as "plug and play" Judaism.

What does "Plug and Play" Judaism mean?

What is Yehoshua claiming about the way North American Jews live their lives? That it is superficial or not authentic? That Israelis live more Jewish lives because they take part in the daily decisions of the Jewish state? Is studying text less Jewish than deciding whether to disengage from Gaza? How would you respond to someone who said "well, you're not a real Jew anyway"

Can you live in a country and not be loyal to it? Can Yehoshua really expect Diaspora Jews not to be loyal to countries in which they reside?

In brief, Yehoshua's remarks caused a highly emotional stir in both Israel and America with their candid and harsh statements. Critics and supporters spoke up, igniting a fire of written responses eventually published into one dialogue of many opinions by the AJC. The resulting debate, taken by storm in Israel, has provoked heated and interesting discussion both of the reality of American Jewish life and how Israel and American Jewry need to relate to one another. On the one hand, he negated all efforts of his audience- those committed to educated and strengthening American ties to Israel- as futile. On the other hand, his remarks resonated "classic Zionism" that Jews and Judaism would thrive best within our own sovereignty and the new reality of Israel's shift from a once struggling nation to thriving, self sufficient, successful democratic state. Wherever you stand on the Yehoshua spectrum, his remarks became a challenge – a dialogue- between Israel and the Diaspora to publicly discuss the reality of the Israel-Diaspora relationship and what it means to be a Jew living in and outside of Israel. The challenge Yeshoshua and the respondents to his comments made for Diaspora Jews was to seriously ponder this issue and be constantly aware of where Israel and Judaism fit in our lives as Jews who call home and homeland different names.

What bothered you, if anything, about his remarks?

Reactions and responses materialized in print, on blogs, and in public discourse. Some of which are included below.

Response 1: Dr. Steven Bayme "Israel and the Diaspora: A Post-Yehoshua Response"

The return of the Jews to sovereignty and statehood constitutes the single greatest success narrative of modern Jewish history. To be a Jew in the twenty-first century necessitates a relationship with the Jewish state. Yet, sadly, Yehoshua is correct in charging American Jews with failure… [there is] an increased detachment from Israel among American Jews… Perhaps the best evidence of the detachment lies in the fact that fewer than 40 percent of the most affluent Jewish community in history has ever set foot in the Jewish state over the first six decades of her existence. Yet Yehoshua erred in trivializing American Judaism…Rather than advocate synergy between Israel and the Diaspora in an effort to enhance the collective Jewish future, he effectively challenges American Jews either to move to Israel and become serious Jews, or stay in the Diaspora and continue to "play with Jewishness."

Dr. Steven Bayme is the director of the Dorothy and Julius Koppelman Institute on American-Jewish- Israeli relations at the American Jewish Committee.

Can you be a committed Jew today without any connection to Israel?

Why do you think so many North American Jews are detached from Israel?

Do you agree with him when he says that a growing disconnection from Israel is part of a distancing from everything else Jewish?

Do you think if the political situation was more secure, that North American Jews would be more attached to Israel and more inclined to go, or is the political instability an excuse?

What factors would encourage more American Jews to go to Israel?

Yossi Beilin is a Knesset member and Chair of the Meretz-Yachad Party

Response 2: Yossi Beilin- "First and Foremost a Jew"

...Then, too, the remarks were interpreted as an Israeli desire to disengage, heaven forbid, from Diaspora Jewry, instead of being understood as an almost desperate call to work together to ensure the continued existence of the Jewish people, rather than making do with sending checks to people who can exist perfectly well without them.

... in order to ensure Jewish continuity in a world that, for all its anti-Semitic phenomena, is prepared to smile at Jews in a way it has never before smiled, and where a Jewish spouse is not a disaster but often even a great blessing. Immigration to Israel is the most effective solution, but it is practical only for very few in the wealthy countries. When I initiated the birthright project, I did this in the conviction that Israel must be a meeting point for the Jewish people as part of the effort to ensure Jewish continuity.

Do you see Israel as a "Jewish meeting point?" How else would you define it for the Jewish People?

Which other issues can we discuss in terms of Jewish continuity both in the Israeli and Diaspora Jewish communities?

What do the two communities have in common and how do their issues in terms of Jewish continuity differ?

Ze'ev Bielski is the chairman of the Jewish Agency and the World Zionist Organization

Response 3: Ze'ev Bielski- "Disconnected from Reality"

I find Yehoshua's statement disconnected from the existential reality of the Jewish people. More than half of the Jewish people live in Israel. The state is perceived by the Jewish community in the Diaspora as a strong and established state, not as a weak state just starting out, connected as it was in the past by an umbilical cord to Diaspora Jewry, and dependent upon it.

We are working to strengthen the "attractive" elements of Israel, but in the absence of significant factors that help "push" them, most Jews in the Diaspora, particularly in the United States, choose to remain where they are. The lives of many of them are connected to Israel. They contribute to it generously and are involved in many joint projects

They regard the connection with Israel as the primary means for connecting their children with Jewish tradition, culture and values, with the assets of Jewish culture and community life, and particularly as a means for guaranteeing their continued lives as Jews.

How is Israel used as a "primary means for connecting their children with Jewish tradition, culture and values, with the assets of Jewish culture and community life, and particularly as a means for guaranteeing their continued lives as Jews?"

How do you connect with Israel as part of your Jewish identity?

In what ways do you demonstrate your connection?

Activity: The Great Debate

If AB Yehoshua was in front of you right now, what would you say to him? Yehoshua's remarks sparked great controversy and a major debate erupted in the Israeli and American Jewish communities. Imagine you were able to sit down and schmooze with Yehoshua. How would you respond to his remarks and answer the following questions:

1. Does Israel need North American Jewry?
2. How Can North American Jews Contribute to the Jewish State?
3. Can Israel survive without North American financial, political and moral support?
4. What does Israel offer North American Jewry that they can't experience in North America?
5. How can we find common ground and shared interests?
6. How can we prove to both Israelis are North American Jews that we are one people and have a collective fate tied to Israel?
7. How has Israel's existence made your Jewish life richer and how can we share this message?

Ideas to consider: The notion of Peoplehood and Jewish unity, safety, continuity of the North American Jewish communities, joint responsibility for Jewish continuity and Jewish civilization, shared interests, commonalities and differences.

We no longer face the physical threats we once did, however, we are facing a different kind of threat.— that of assimilation. If Israel was the answer to providing a safe haven for Jews in need, what then is the answer to the problem of assimilation?
Look at the remarks below on this page. What about that person's remarks do you connect with? How would you define the past and future relationship between Israel and North American Jews?

Leonard Fein, founder Moment Magazine and Mazon: The Jewish Response to Hunger:
"The Jewish people has by now 'lost' as many people to assimilation as it did to slaughter... the argument about Zionism comes down to an argument about Jewishness...if Judaism amounts to no more than Israeliness, then we here are meaningless as Jews...Zionism must...somehow include a link between the Jewish state and the Jewish people"

Tzivia Greenfield, head of Mifne Institute for Democracy and Judaism:
"there is a point to Jewish continuity only if it entails taking complete responsibility...for all aspects of our lives...this collective responsibility...includes ... the shared concern for our for the continued existence and physical flourishing of the inhabitants of Israel"

Alfred H. Moses, past president of the AJC, Chair of Centennial Committee:
"I agree that there is a threat to Jewish existence in the Diaspora and this internal danger, the danger of apathy is greater than the external danger that threatens the Jewish existence in Israel. The religious people in the Diaspora will remain Jewish. The problem is with the secular-civic society. A Jewish uniqueness is essential for Jewish survival...the fact that we live in a non-Jewish environment has advantages but also has a cost...Israel and Diaspora communities are mutually dependent. The very existence of Israel for better or worse, is dependent on the United States. The Europeans will shed many tears at Israel's funeral but won't do anything to prevent it. The only country that is obligated to prevent Israel's destruction and that will act to do so is the United States"

Activity: How do you see Israel?

In 1967, when Israel triumphed in the Six-Day War, Israel was seen as indestructible and there was a strong sense of support for Israel. In the 1980's, the feelings became some-what blasé. Now, in the 21st century, there is a revival of Israel education. The older generation experienced the thrills of independence, the tension and drama of the military victory of 1967.The younger generation's formative experiences have been war, intifada and terrorism and *"as a result, their Israel is very different from that of their parents and grand-parents"*

Compare the two views on Israel and determine where you stand. How do you see Israel fitting in to your Jewish identity? What do you want Israel to be for your generation?

GENERATION ONE	MY ISRAEL	GENERATION TWO
Israel is primarily experienced as a vital and dynamic place.		Israel is primarily experienced as a dying and desperate place.
Israel is more about me and the future, then my parents and the past.		Israel is more about my parents' & grandparents' generations than about me.
Israelis are young, strong and sexy—they convey a totally different and appealing image of what it is to be a Jew today.		Israelis are arrogant, aggressive and even unethical.
Unlike my parents, grandparents and generations of Jews going back throughout history, I can actually go freely to Israel.		It's no big deal for me to go. Visiting Israel doesn't make me feel like a pioneer.
Israel enables me to draw a remarkable connection between Judaism, the land and the text.		My connection to the land is undermined by the decline of socialism, the Kibbutz movement and the media and revisionists who challenge the sacredness of the land
I feel totally connected to all the faces on the bus— everyone's Jewish here.		I feel suspicious of the people on the bus— who is the terrorist?
Israel embodies Jewish community. In America, community is starting to dwindle; in Israel it is vibrant.		The community spirit of the kibbutz model is outdated— even to Israelis.
Israel is Jewish time and Jewish space as lived by a Jewish majority.		The idea of a Jewish majority lies in direct conflict with more widely accepted liberal ideas of pluralism and multiculturalism.
Israel ties me into Jewish history— I feel like I'm part of the Jewish historical collective here, and I'm participating in the unfolding of the story of the Jewish people.		Creating a Jewish state was thrilling. War and persecution of minorities loses its appeal.
Judaism is alive in Israel— you can join thousands of people on a Shavuot pilgrimage to Jerusalem; you can feel the sanctity of Yom Kippur simply by walking through the streets.		Judaism is coercive in Israel and questions my right to practice my type of Judaism.

Philosopher's Retreat: Appendix 1 , Makom: The Israel Engagemnt Network—www.makomisrael.net

What is the place of Israel for North American Jews?

The Philosopher's Retreat

In September 2003, Alan Hoffmann, the Director General of the Jewish Agency's educational Department, convened a small group of philosophers, educators, and community lay leaders to begin a process to explore the place of Israel in contemporary American Jewish life. It was an attempt to capture and make widely available an assessment of the state of the field of Israel engagement.

In the 1960's, 70's and 80's, following a successful military victory of the 1967 Six-Day War in Israel, Jews in the Diaspora worked hard to build a sense of Jewish unity around Israel's plight. In the 1990's, the conversations in the Diaspora started to shift to a more positive and value-based campaign. We did start to see a significant decline in the levels of attachment to Israel, but it wasn't until the outbreak of the Intifada that the repercussions of those trends were fully felt. Jews were confused about their attachment to Israel and, in contrast to what happened in 1967, Diaspora Jewry stopped visiting Israel. Anti-Israel sentiment in the media and on the university campus resulted in a rise of anti-Semitism- particularly in Europe- brought about new challenges and difficulties for Jews everywhere. Jewish college students were poorly equipped to deal with anti-Israel sentiment. Israel found herself once again in the hearts and mind of worldwide Jewry and the Jewish educational world jumped at the opportunity to enter the conversation again.

The traditional Zionist paradigm was under attack – the notions of Israel as the safe haven for the Jewish People, the solution to anti-Semitism, the ingatherer of the exiles, the savior of Judaism and Jewish culture, etc., were all being questioned, not only in the Diaspora, but in the State of Israel itself. The classical notions of Zionism were being questioned. For two days, they discussed the philosophical relationship between Israel and American Jewry, in both its historical and contemporary contexts.

Does this shift in the meaning of Zionism mean the end of it? Where do we go from here given the current realties?

What can we say about the guiding foundations of Israel that remain as powerful today as they were in 1948?
Three core pillars were identified:
1) Israel is the only place in the world where the Jewish People has decided to take its political fate into its own hands;
2) Israel is the only place in the world in which total Jewish space exists;
3) Israel is the only place in the world that creates the possibility of a vibrant Hebrew culture.

The question that immediately emerged was whether Diaspora Jews could be involved in any way in any of these three pillars. If these are the three principles upon which Israel stands and Diaspora Jewry has no direct involvement with any of them, this formulation might simply represent a conversation stopper.

Excerpted from "The Philospher's Retreat", 2004. Makom: The Israel Engagemnt Network— www.makomisrael.net

How you think that Diaspora Jews could be involved in any way in any of the three pillars mentioned above? What would be the pros and cons of the involvement?

_____

_____

_____

Does Israel need North American Jewry?

How can North American Jews contribute to the Jewish State? Four levels of contribution were suggested in the Philosopher's Retreat:

1) Israel needs American Jewry's support – indeed, this is a life and death issue. Without American Jewish financial, political and moral support, it is questionable whether Israel can survive.
2) We ought to be working towards the notion of Peoplehood, and the idea that we will be recognizable as one people.
3) America needs Israel to ensure the continuity of the American Jewish community.
4) American Jewry is a source of demographic potential for Israel.

Perhaps the bottom line is that the Jewish People, both in Israel and the Diaspora, have a joint responsibility for the reproduction, deepening and enrichment of Jewish civilization.

What other ways do you think North American Jews can contribute to the Jewish state?

_____

_____

_____

_____

Challenging the pillars

Are the three pillars outlined above correct? As the participants in the retreat reflected on the earlier thesis, a critique began to emerge. It was argued that the first of the pillars – taking fate into our own hands in our own land – is actually a somewhat mythical notion. The State of Israel is not entirely in control of its own destiny; **indeed, it is significantly dependent upon the American government and the American Jewish community.** It is certainly easy to argue that the existence of the State of Israel gives the Jewish People more power than they have had in at least two millennia, but it would be incorrect to assume that the fate and destiny of the Jewish People is now totally in the hands of the State of Israel.

Furthermore, we should not necessarily assume that political self reliance is the best strategy to maintain the future of the Jewish People – there is a tendency today to assume that it is, but a strong critique of Zionism existed in the first half of the twentieth century, and has certainly started to reemerge in recent years. The dominant view – in the Jewish world and around the retreat table – was that the idea of a strong, Jewish, self reliant entity is certainly a good thing, but it was argued that it is always important to consider the cost of self reliance. Part of Israel education ought to involve recognition of the fact that **self reliance means paying a very serious price; we should continually seek to learn what that price is, and recall why we were and are willing to pay it.**

The second pillar – the creation of total Jewish public space – is also somewhat problematic. Israel is certainly a different space from the Diaspora, but the notion that it is a singular and all encompassing Jewish public space no longer holds (if it indeed ever did), **because there are so many different expressions of Jewishness that exist there.**

Excerpted from "The Philospher's Retreat", 2004. Makom: The Israel Engagemnt Network— www.makomisrael.net

And the third pillar – the creation of a vibrant Hebrew culture – was also considered inaccurate. While there is certainly a continuum of Hebrew culture from Bialik to Agnon to Amichai and beyond, **Israel today is actually a multi-cultural space.** It is not simply the place where a singular vibrant Jewish culture develops; **it is also a place where other cultures exist and grow.**

Following the critique, the three pillars could be rewritten as follows:

"Israel has taken upon itself a great historical responsibility – to create one place in the world...
1) ...where the Jewish People benefits from, and pays the price for its attempt to take its political fate into its own hands;
2) ...where Jewish public spaces exist;
3) ...that creates the possibility of vibrant Hebrew cultures.

How could you re-write the three pillars to better explain them?

Are we only Zionists when we are safe? Does Zionism survive the test of insecurity, vulnerability and terrorism?

How can you feel attached to Israel but not to Judaism? Do you know any people who are strong Zionists, but not religiously connected at all? Can you have one without the other?

Activity: Israeli or Jewish?

Think about what you know about life in Israel. Is everything Israeli, Jewish? When a convention of Jews gathers, what is Jewish about it?

List five things that are specifically Jewish and five that are Israel. Jot down, if any, ones that overlap

	Jewish	Israeli	Could be both
1.			
2.			
3.			
4.			
5.			

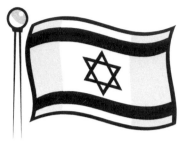

Tefillah L'shlom Hamedinah: Prayer for the State of Israel
תפילה לשלום המדינה

In some synagogues one can find many different Siddurim, yet the differences between them are very slight. There is one prayer, however, in which the differences are enormous. The original prayer was composed in 1949 by the Chief Rabbinate to include the new State in modern liturgy. Different congregations use this prayer in different ways- some include it everyday, some just on Shabbat, some say both Hebrew and English, some just recite the Hebrew and some congregations do not include it at all in their service. The Siddur Sim Shalom, includes it near the end of the Torah service, *following* the Prayer for Our Country.

As we look at the differences in the versions, we see that most are based upon ideological differences concerning the State of Israel and its place in Jewish life.

The tefillah has four main sections— state and its leadership, defense, well being of Jews worldwide and Israel as the Jewish homeland, and a statement of God's supreme authority.

Why was there a need to create a prayer for Israel to be included in modern liturgy?

Should Jews in the Diaspora formally pray for Israel?

What does this prayer mean to you?

Prayer written by the Chief Rabbis of Israel in 1949

אָבִינוּ שֶׁבַּשָּׁמַיִם, צוּר יִשְׂרָאֵל וְגוֹאֲלוֹ, בָּרֵךְ אֶת מְדִינַת יִשְׂרָאֵל, רֵאשִׁית צְמִיחַת גְּאֻלָּתֵנוּ. הָגֵן עָלֶיהָ בְּאֶבְרַת חַסְדֶּךָ וּפְרוֹשׂ עָלֶיהָ סֻכַּת שְׁלוֹמֶךָ, וּשְׁלַח אוֹרְךָ וַאֲמִתְּךָ לְרָאשֶׁיהָ, שָׂרֶיהָ וְיוֹעֲצֶיהָ, וְתַקְּנֵם בְּעֵצָה טוֹבָה מִלְּפָנֶיךָ. חַזֵּק אֶת יְדֵי מְגִנֵּי אֶרֶץ קָדְשֵׁנוּ, וְהַנְחִילֵם אֱלֹהֵינוּ יְשׁוּעָה, וַעֲטֶרֶת נִצָּחוֹן תְּעַטְּרֵם, וְנָתַתָּ שָׁלוֹם בָּאָרֶץ, וְשִׂמְחַת עוֹלָם לְיוֹשְׁבֶיהָ.

וְאֶת אַחֵינוּ כָּל בֵּית יִשְׂרָאֵל פְּקָד נָא בְּכָל אַרְצוֹת פְּזוּרֵיהֶם, וְתוֹלִיכֵם מְהֵרָה קוֹמְמִיּוּת לְצִיּוֹן עִירֶךָ וְלִירוּשָׁלַיִם מִשְׁכַּן שְׁמֶךָ, כַּכָּתוּב בְּתוֹרַת מֹשֶׁה עַבְדֶּךָ: אִם יִהְיֶה נִדַּחֲךָ בִּקְצֵה הַשָּׁמַיִם, מִשָּׁם יְקַבֶּצְךָ יְיָ אֱלֹהֶיךָ וּמִשָּׁם יִקָּחֶךָ. וֶהֱבִיאֲךָ יְיָ אֱלֹהֶיךָ אֶל הָאָרֶץ אֲשֶׁר יָרְשׁוּ אֲבֹתֶיךָ וִירִשְׁתָּהּ, וְהֵיטִבְךָ וְהִרְבְּךָ מֵאֲבֹתֶיךָ. וְיַחֵד לְבָבֵנוּ לְאַהֲבָה וּלְיִרְאָה אֶת שְׁמֶךָ, וְלִשְׁמֹר אֶת כָּל דִּבְרֵי תוֹרָתֶךָ, וּשְׁלַח לָנוּ מְהֵרָה בֶּן דָּוִד מְשִׁיחַ צִדְקֶךָ, לִפְדוֹת מְחַכֵּי קֵץ יְשׁוּעָתֶךָ. הוֹפַע בַּהֲדַר גְּאוֹן עֻזֶּךָ עַל כָּל יוֹשְׁבֵי תֵבֵל אַרְצֶךָ, וְיֹאמַר כֹּל אֲשֶׁר נְשָׁמָה בְאַפּוֹ, יְיָ אֱלֹהֵי יִשְׂרָאֵל מֶלֶךְ וּמַלְכוּתוֹ בַּכֹּל מָשָׁלָה, אָמֵן סֶלָה.

Our Father in Heaven, Rock and Redeemer of Israel, Bless the State of Israel, the beginning of our redemption. Shelter it under the wings of Thy love. Spread over it the Tabernacle of Thy Peace. Grant Thy light and truth to its leaders, ministers and advisors and inspire them with good counsel. Support the defenders of our sacred land: Grant them deliverance. O our God and crown them with victory Grant peace in our land and lasting joy to its inhabitants.

Remember Thou our brothers all the house of Israel in all the lands of the Dispersion. Lead them, swiftly and upright, to Your city Zion and to Jerusalem, the abode of Your Name, as is written in the Torah of Your servant Moses: "Even if your outcasts are at the ends of the world, from there the Lord your God will gather you, from there He will fetch you. And the Lord your God will bring you to the land that your fathers possessed, and you shall possess it; and He will make you more prosperous and more numerous than your fathers." Draw our hearts together to revere and venerate Your name and to observe all the precepts of Your Torah, and send us quickly the Messiah son of David, agent of Your vindication, to redeem those who await Your deliverance. Manifest yourself in the splendor of Your boldness before the eyes of all inhabitants of Your world, and may everyone endowed with a soul affirm that the Lord, God of Israel, is king and his dominion is absolute. Amen forevermore.

Activity: Explore the Tefillah

Read both the English and Hebrew of the tefillah. Pick 2-3 central themes of the prayer.

Themes:

What is it asking of God?

What types of familiar "prayer" words do you recognize?

How do we refer to the state of Israel?

A major aspect of the prayer is Geulah- Redemption.

What are the signs of redemption? Has the establishment of Israel brought us any closer to the Geulah?

Should the prayer for Israel deal with mankind and more universal concepts?

Why do you think a Prayer for the State of Israel was incorporated into Diaspora liturgy?

How does this prayer express the centrality of Israel in the lives of Diaspora Jews? What other focus does it have?

What does this text *really* say?

What meaning does that have for Diaspora Jews and do we really mean what we say when we recite this prayer?

Now read the version that it is the Siddur Sim Shalom:

Siddur Sim Shalom

אָבִינוּ שֶׁבַּשָּׁמַיִם, צוּר יִשְׂרָאֵל וְגוֹאֲלוֹ, בָּרֵךְ אֶת מְדִינַת יִשְׂרָאֵל, רֵאשִׁית צְמִיחַת גְּאֻלָּתֵנוּ.
הָגֵן עָלֶיהָ בְּאֶבְרַת חַסְדֶּךָ וּפְרֹס עָלֶיהָ סֻכַּת שְׁלוֹמֶךָ, וּשְׁלַח אוֹרְךָ וַאֲמִתְּךָ לְרָאשֶׁיהָ, שָׂרֶיהָ
וְיוֹעֲצֶיהָ, וְתַקְּנֵם בְּעֵצָה טוֹבָה מִלְּפָנֶיךָ. חַזֵּק אֶת יְדֵי מְגִנֵּי אֶרֶץ קָדְשֵׁנוּ, וְהַנְחִילֵם אֱלֹהֵינוּ
יְשׁוּעָה, וַעֲטֶרֶת נִצָּחוֹן תְּעַטְּרֵם, וְנָתַתָּ שָׁלוֹם בָּאָרֶץ, וְשִׂמְחַת עוֹלָם לְיוֹשְׁבֶיהָ.

*Our Father in Heaven, Rock and Redeemer of the people Israel; Bless the State of Is-
rael, with its promise of redemption. Shield it with Your love; spread over it the shelter
of Your peace. Guide its leaders and advisors with Your light and Your truth. Help them
with Your good counsel. Strengthen the hands of those who defend our Holy Land. Deliver them; crown their efforts with triumph. Bless the land with peace, and its inhabitants with lasting joy. And let us say: Amen.*

What was removed from the original text? Why?

Underline or circle controversial words or phrases in the original text. Why would these
words cause discomfort among Conservative Jews? Record controversial words or phrases
and give reasons why:

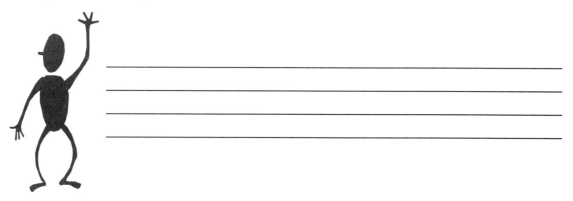

Do you think this prayer is appropriately placed *following* the *Prayer for Our Country*? Is this
making a statement that we are (North) American first and foremost and our allegiance to
Israel is secondary? Do you think the different versions symbolize the ideological differences between North American Jews?

Why would some congregations choose NOT to pray for Israel in a formal prayer setting?

What does the shortened version in the Sim Shalom say about the different ways Diaspora
Jews relate to Israel?

Tikvateinu—Our Hope

"Hatikvah" ("The Hope") is the national anthem of the State of Israel. It was composed by Naphtali Herz Imber and originally published under the title "Tikvateinu" ("Our Hope") in 1886. About four years before it was published, the words of "Hatikvah" were set to a melody, which had acquired the familiarity of a folk song. "Hatikvah" was introduced as a possible anthem in 1901 at the Fifth Zionist Conference. By the Seventh Zionist Congress in 1905, everyone knew "Hatikvah" and ended the meeting with a communal singing of it. "Hatikvah" did not receive official recognition as the Zionist anthem until the 18th Zionist Congress in 1933.

התקוה

כל עוד בלבב פנימה
נפש יהודי הומיה
ולפאתי מזרח קדימה
עין לציון צופיה
עוד לא אבדה תקותנו
התקוה בת שנות אלפים
להיות עם חופשי בארצנו
ארץ ציון וירושלים

As long as within our hearts
The Jewish soul sings,
As long as forward to the East
To Zion, looks the eye -
Our hope is not yet lost,
It is two thousand years old,
To be a free people in our land
The land of Zion and Jerusalem.

If you could re-write HaTikvah, what would it say?
Does the Hatikvah include everything it should?
Write a few lines expressing your own hope for Israel and the Jewish people.

_____

_____

_____

_____

Can you imagine what it is like to hope and dream about something for 2000 years? Do you hope for the same things now that you did when you were little?
In what way is Hatikva a prayer?
Why is "east" so important? What is the hope that is referred to in this song?

Why do you think this is the hope? Do you think the hope has changed? If so, what is the hope now? How would you define "hope" based on the lyrics of "Hatikvah"? Upon what is this hope conditional? What specific hope does "Hatikvah" describe?

What is the meaning of the phrase "to be free in our own land"? Do you think it means something different to an Israeli than it does to an American or Canadian?

This song was written many decades before Israel became a sovereign state. Has the hope of the song been fulfilled? If not, what work remains? If yes, what is the meaning of the song today?